The
Growing
Vocabulary

Fun and Adventure with Words

Dr. Archibald Hart
has also written

Twelve Ways to Build A Vocabulary

Comment

"This book on vocabulary building is a notable contribution to the text books in its field because of the highly selective character of the material presented."—*Elementary English Review*

"This little book really is as pleasant to use as if it were one of the games that has captivated the American public."—*Quill and Scroll*

"Dr. Hart...has given us a book which, far from having any of the dust of the classroom about it, actually is as stimulating as a ride on a roller coaster."—*Better English*

"This is a sane treatment of vocabulary building, thoroughly and interestingly presented."—*The Tennessee Speech Journal*

"A notable contribution to the textbooks in it's field. No teacher can become acquainted with this book without self-improvement in vocabulary, and no successful teacher, alert to the vocabulary problems of her children, will fail to adapt the materials to their needs."—*C.C.Certain, The Elementary English Review*

"I can highly recommend it heartily for use with freshman classes. I can also recommend it to the more mature person who for practical or cultural reasons wishes to improve his command of English."
—*Thomas O. Mabbott, Assoc. Prof of English, Hunter College*

The Growing Vocabulary

Fun and Adventure with Words

By

ARCHIBALD HART, PH.D.

Principal of the Home Instruction Division
Calvert School

and

F. ARNOLD LEJEUNE.

Headmaster, The Crane Country Day School,
Santa Barbara, California

With an Introduction by
OSCAR H. MCPHERSON
Librarian,, The Lawrenceville School,
Lawrenceville, New Jersey

Printed by permission

Calvert Education Services
Hunt Valley, Maryland 21031
USA

PRINTED IN THE UNITED STATES OF AMERICA
2003

Contents

The Growing Vocabulary

PART TWO

Contents

The Growing Vocabulary

PART FOUR

Contents

Authors' Preface

This book is designed to help those who are awakening to the pleasure, beauty and power of words. It will appeal especially, perhaps, to boys and girls from about twelve to sixteen; but since it deals with the most flexible and fluent of human creations and since at any age one may catch the fascination of words and of the thoughts that lie behind words, an intelligent child of nine or ten may find something amusing in the earlier parts of the book, and a mature man or woman will find pleasure in the latter sections.

The book is constructed in four parts of progressive difficulty. Though the authors have not adhered slavishly to any list of words, they are indebted to E.L.Thorndike's painstaking measurement of word frequencies in over ten million words of reading matter*.

The obvious way to use this book is to move forward through its pages, progressing rapidly until one finds the sections increasing in difficulty and then slowing to engage in deliberate vocabulary building. A glance at the Table of Contents, however, will suggest another method. Many of the devices for increasing vocabulary, it will be found, recur several times, and all sections which

---

* See the *Thorndike–Century Junior Dictionary,* published by Scott, Foresman and Company.

approach the problem in the same way are numbered systematically to facilitate skipping through the book from one section to the next of the same kind. "Families or Words," for instance, is the title of Sections 1, 11, 21, 31, and 41 and "How Many Do You Know?" appears as the title of Sections 7, 17, 27, 37, 47, 57, and 67. At the end of each section in a series there has been placed a note sending the reader on to the next.

As auxiliaries to the profitable use of *The Growing Vocabulary* the authors wish to recommend the following practices:

1. Frequent reference to a good dictionary;
2. The use of some serviceable book of synonyms, such as Roget's *Thesaurus*;
3. Keeping of a personal list of new words, with their definitions. This list may be kept in a notebook or even on loose sheets of paper; but more effective is the use of a pack of three-by- five- inch index cards. The unfamiliar word should be written on the front of the card; on the reverse should be written a brief definition and, wherever possible, a phrase or sentence containing the word in context. One should review the cards frequently, setting aside those words which are easily learned and concentrating only on the troublesome ones. It is encouraging to see one's pile of mastered words growing.

A.H.

F.A.L

Santa Barbara, California
July 25, 1940.

Introduction

In January, 1939, the present publishers issued Dr. Hart's *Twelve Ways to Build a Vocabulary*. Six more printings, three of them of a "New, Revised Edition," had appeared by the end of November. There was a real demand for the book, both from the general public and from the schools. If I were a publisher, particularly a publisher of such a book, that would offer me reason enough to try another much like the first but with additions, subtractions, and other changes growing of reactions to the first.

But I am not a publisher, merely a school librarian, a person supposed to live on and feed to others the fat of the publishing land. *Twelve Ways* had given me and many of my charges nourishing, palatable fare. To change the figure, it was doing what I had long theretofore been trying to find books to do: persuade young quasi-literates to make themselves more aptly literate the hard way. This book did just that and often not only made them like it but find it irresistible.

It was therefore with much hesitation that I promised to write an introduction to the present book, only if, on reading the manuscript, I felt that it was even better than the other. It is with real enthusiasm that I keep my promise.

The librarian may, if he is fortunate, provide the meat in the sandwich pedagogic offered the pupil in every good secondary school. The bread is sliced from the respective loaves, curriculum and extra-curriculum. He should be a dietician, ready to analyze appetites of the minds, personalities, and tastes of his young friends, and to persuade them to be willing eaters of the foods that will make up respective deficiencies in vitamins. To him all scholastic departments have treasures of value equal each to each but equal also to those of each extra-curricular field. He must evaluate these offerings separately for the individuals he is guiding.

But he should be able as well to give more of the food craved by every young mind or spirit. He should be able even to create such a craving in those who lack it. He should, in other words, try to make each pupil strong where he is weak and stronger where he is strong.

What is true of school librarians, opening eyes that may be seeing for the first time, is at least as true of readers' advisers in public libraries. They, in these exciting days of adult education, are, more than ever before, opening or reopening eyes that, for whatever reason, have been closed.

But all who use books as a medium of education, librarians, teachers, parents, find one handicap far too common and too often apparently hopeless among their protégés: verbal inadequacy. If the child or adult has not learned to read or write effectively, he will not open books willingly. For many, *Twelve Ways* has been invaluable in starting the process that is overcoming that common handicap, particularly when each person most concerned has had his own copy, for unlimited use. It has often been self-starting. It has subtly whetted the appetite for more. It has developed the taste for good dictionaries. It has been habit-forming.

The Growing Vocabulary gives convincing promise of doing all that and more, with greater simplicity, directness, aptness, subtlety, and hence with greater effectiveness.

OSCAR H. MCPHERSON

The Richest Language

One may picture the English language as a treasure-house crowded with the riches of many centuries. Here for fourteen hundred years an influx of raiders, conquerors, priests, missionaries, travelers, scholars, merchants, scientists, humorists, pedants, dilettantes, and returned explorers have made their deposits; and here many of their riches still remain free to the hand of the gatherer. Anyone beginning the study of words will wish to know something of the history of the many words at his disposal.

In the years preceding 449 A.D. certain Germanic tribes living near the mouth of the Elbe and along the southwest coast of the Baltic spoke a dialect of German. In that year these tribes—the Angles, the Saxons, and the Jutes—began to raid the south coast of England, and eventually driving the natives into the mountains, proceeded to establish themselves and their language. For six hundred years or more their Germanic dialect, now called Anglo-Saxon or Old English, was the English language, and from that language some two thousand common words like *land, day, way, life, foot, care, man, bless, ghost, God, heaven, king, answer, ordeal, starboard,* and *darling* have lived on to be a part of modern English.

Latin added to the slender word-store of Anglo-Saxon. The Romans who had come with Caesar in 55 B.C. and who remained in England during more than four centuries until they withdrew to defend Rome in 410 had left a few Latin words such as *lake, mount, street, wall*, and *wine*. Other Latin words came to England with missionaries in the seventh century—*monk, clerk, altar, bishop, priest, psalm, lily, plant, pine, trout, lobster, butter, cheese, cup, dish, inch, kitchen,* and *sickle*. Raiding Danes contributed words like *sky, fellow, haven, knife, husband, wrong,* and *law*.

But these deposits in the treasure-house of the English language were as nothing compared with the enrichment that began about 1100 and persisted until Shakespeare's day. In 1066 William the Conqueror invaded England and brought with him the French language. This language, being the tongue of the newly established aristocracy and of the conquering race, slowly began to exert its influence upon the vocabulary of "English" as it was then constituted; by Chaucer's time (1340-1400) the language sounded and looked almost French because of the hundreds of French words that had been taken over and added to the native tongue. Some of the thousands of words borrowed from French and still remaining are *miracle, adroit, brunette, cajole, chagrin. forest, duke, castle, justice, privilege, court, tower, treason, campaign, battle, peace,* and other words connected with law, warfare, architecture, and the life of an aristocratic society.

Later our language took on words from many languages

other than French. Spain and Italy gave England such words as *mosquito, armada, flotilla, vanilla, alligator,* and *brigand, ducat, balcony, pilgrim, dilettante, campanile, cameo, catacomb, piano.* Holland and Germany contributed *skate* and *zinc*; Portuguese added *banana, cocoa, binnacle*; Arabic gave *admiral, alkali, algebra, coffee, cotton*; and the American Indian sent across the Atlantic such words as *moose, moccasin, squaw, toboggan,* and *tomahawk.*

More than two hundred million people now speak English. Our own language in the United States is a sort of dialect of English, a flourishing branch developed from the root stock. Language is always changing, and a hundred and fifty years has been enough to enable us to take on new words, new inflections, new idioms, and new pronunciations. "Good" English, particularly in its written form, still tends to remain close to the language of British literature, though even in our literary writing, we have developed a way of expressing ourselves which is perceptibly different from the British way. Certain differences in the British and American vocabularies are discussed in Sections 77, 87, and 97 of this book.

The
Growing
Vocabulary

Fun and Adventure with Words

Part One

1
Families of Words

Words often occur in families. For instance, it is obvious at a glance that *glory, glorious, glorify,* and *glorification* must be related; so are *fraternal, fraternity,* and *fraternize*; and *revoke, revocable,* and *revocation.*

If you know one of the members of a family, it is easy to make acquaintance with the others. Often, merely by learning a single unfamiliar word, you will come to know three of four others that are closely related. Suppose, for example, that until today you had not known the meaning of *prefer*; wouldn't it be easy, once you had learned the word, to understand the meaning of *preference, preferable, preferably,* and even *preferment?*

Here are a few common families of words. You will probably find that you already know the first word of each family and perhaps some of the others. If there are any members of a family that are unfamiliar to you, become acquainted at once.

Don't guess! Look up in a dictionary all words which are unknown to you or about which you are doubtful.

Use each word in a sentence of your own composition:

(a) persuade, persuasion, persuasive

(b) unite, unity, unify, unification

(c) perpetual, perpetuate, perpetuity

(d) destroy, destruction, destructive, destroyer, destructible

(e) conspire, conspiracy, conspirator

Gathering families of words is fun. If you enjoyed this section, you may want to turn at once to Section 11, next one which deals with Families or Words.

2

Ten Words from
Alice in Wonderland, by Lewis Carroll

Some boys and girls of ten or eleven, strangely enough, think that *Alice in Wonderland* is too childish for them; yet a great many adults read *Alice* with pleasure and new understanding. Sometimes the vocabulary is not so simple as you might suppose.

Below are some sentences from *Alice in Wonderland*. Rewrite these sentences, substituting a word or phrase of your own for each of the italicized words. Do not change the meaning of the original sentence.

Alice had not the slightest idea what *latitude* was, or *longitude* either, but she thought that they were nice grand words to say.

This bottle was not marked "poison," so Alice *ventured* to taste it.

"In that case," said the Dodo solemnly, rising to its feet, "I move that the meeting *adjourn*, for the immediate *adoption* of more energetic *remedies*."

Some of the other birds tittered *audibly*.

Here one of the guinea-pigs cheered, and

was immediately *suppressed* by the officers of the court.

The first question of course was, how to get dry again; they had a *consultation* about this, and after a few minutes it seemed quite natural to Alice to find herself talking *familiarly* with them.

See if you can find any more words in *Alice* whose meanings you do not know. How about *quadrille*?

3

Synonyms

When two words have almost the same meaning, like *begin* and *commence*, they are called "synonyms." The English language is rich in pairs and sets of words that are similar to one another in meaning; it has, to give one example, many words which express the general idea of "large." A large book can also be called big, enormous, huge, gigantic, and ponderous; and in each case you will understand that the book is large.

An effective way to increase the size of your vocabulary is to settle upon some word like *little, old, happy, house,* or *receive* and to search in your mind for synonyms. Write them down, and when you are sure that you can think of no more, ask someone with a larger vocabulary than yours to suggest words that you have missed. As a rule, older people and those who make a habit of reading a good deal will prove to have larger vocabularies than the average boy and girl.

Make written lists of all the words you can think of that are synonyms of:

happy	unhappy
brave	strong

tired	afraid
pretty	little
old	intelligent

In searching for words, don't give up too easily. If you enjoy trying to find synonyms, you will find further opportunities to do so in sections 13, 23, 33, and 43 of this book.

4

Definitions

Suppose someone were to ask you what a boat is. That seems rather an easy question to answer, but perhaps it is not so easy as it sounds.

Try it. Perhaps you will answer that a boat is a hollow object which floats on the water and can be moved by the use of oars or by other means. Have you really described a boat and *nothing else except a boat*? Wouldn't your description fit some other object, a wash tub for instance?

In making your definition of a boat you must try to word it in such a way that it cannot possibly apply to anything except a boat. How is this for the description of a boat? "A boat is a small craft for use on water and designed to carry people and to be propelled by the use of oars, sails, or a small engine." If you can find any error or omission in that definition, rewrite it and improve upon it.

Define the following words. Do not look up the definition of a word in the dictionary until you have made a real effort to form the definition for yourself.

city (be sure you do not include town or
village in your definition)
ocean (be sure that you do not describe a
lake or a river)
book
foolish
generous
old-fashioned
discover
argue
persuade
injure (Don't be content merely to say
that *injure* means *hurt* or *damage*;
give a full statement of the meaning
of *injure*, not just a synonym.)

Sections 14 and 24 continue the discussion of
definitions.

5

Can You Answer These Questions?

(You can do so if you know the meanings of the italicized words.)

(a) What is an *italicized* word?
(b) What is the difference between a *rivulet* and a river?
(c) Why is it almost impossible to hold a *cargo* in your hand?
(d) Why do most people enjoy *leisure*?
(e) Why is *perseverance* usually considered a desirable quality?
(f) Why should a policeman be *alert*?
(g) What happens when a tower *topples*?
(h) Why do most people want to have *endurance*?
(i) Why do you dislike *odious* people?
(j) Why is a *weird* sound seldom funny?

In Section 10 you will find more questions to answer.

6

Ten Words from *Through the Looking-Glass*, by Lewis Carroll

The words in *Through the Looking-Glass* are a little harder than those in *Alice in Wonderland*. Here are ten which may be unfamiliar to you. In a dictionary look up any word that you do not know; then write it in a sentence of your own composition.

She stood silent, watching one of them that was bustling about among the flowers, poking its *proboscis* into them, "just as if it was a regular bee," thought Alice.

All hopping through the *frothy* waves...

"The prettiest are always further!" she said at last with a sigh at the *obstinacy* of the rushes in growing so far off.

You see it's like a *portmanteau*—there are two meanings packed up into one word.

She found the White King seated on the ground, busily writing in his *memorandum-book*.

Alice was sawing away *diligently* with the knife.

The Queen went on in a tone of grave *reproof.*

She did not wait for Alice to *curtsey* this time.

The thing to do was to make a grand *survey* of the country.

Just then a *fawn* came wandering by.

7

How Many Do You Know?

Each word in the first column below has a synonym in the second column. Match the synonyms by considering separately each word in the first column and by finding a word in the second column which corresponds to it.

For example, with *industrious* in mind, run through the second column until you come to a word (or a phrase) that has a similar meaning. In this case the word is *hard-working*. Indicate your answer by writing "industrious—hard-working."

industrious   without ceremony
erroneous   high
elevated   hearty
apprehensive   glorious
cordial   hard-working
informal   stupid
monotonous   expensive
                   wrong
                   fearful
                   sudden
                   rolling
                   not varying

If you enjoy matching synonyms, turn to Section 17, which is like this section.

8

Imitative Words

We do not know how most words originally took on the meanings which they now have. There seems to be no really sound reason why *big* should mean "big" rather than "little" or "red" or "pretty." We all take it for granted, however, that the sound "big" and the letters b-i-g are to mean "large"; consequently there is no confusion. Any other word might do as well as *big* to convey the same meaning, but we settled upon that word rather than another.

The origins of such words, often very old, cannot now be traced. There are other words, however, which mean what they do for a very good reason, and the reason is clear. No other word would convey the meanings so well. These words, like *buzz*, *hum*, and *cackle*, are imitative words which suggest sounds.

Think of all the words that mean, and at the same time imitate, *loud* sounds; you will probably think of words like *clang*, *clatter*, *roar*, *racket*, *hubbub*, *blare*. Use each of these words in a sentence that will show its particular meaning; *blare*, for instance, may be used in a sentence that tells of the blowing of horns or trumpets.

In the same way think of words that mean, and imitate,

soft and gentle sounds like *whisper* and *murmur*:

> (a) Which is louder, the splash of water or the plash of water?
>
> (b) Which is louder, a rustle or rattle?
>
> (c) What word suggests the sound of a large and powerful bell? Of a very small bell?
>
> (d) Think of the sounds which a little brook makes. Which of these words applies best: *roar, gurgle, purl, babble, thunder, ripple*?
>
> Sections 18 and 28 continue the discussion of Imitative Words

9

Good

If you give careful attention to what people say, you will find that a large part of their conversation expresses approval or disapproval of people, actions, and things. You will find that though there are hundreds of ways to say that you like, or approve of, something, almost everyone uses only the word *good*. Such a variety as automobiles, ice-cream sodas, dresses, umpires, books, moving-pictures, houses, vocabularies, dinners and breakfasts, baseball players, radio programs, and thousands of other objects, people and actions are described as "good."

There is nothing "wrong" with the word *good*; but it is dull and lazy to use it many times in the course of a day's talking when one might better use a more accurate, meaningful, and colorful word. Try for a week, whenever you write or talk, to find some word more precise and expressive than *good*; such an attempt will help you form a valuable habit. Meanwhile here are a few questions to help you start:

(a) What makes an automobile "good"? Rather than saying that an automobile is good, wouldn't it be preferable to say that is is fast, speedy, good-looking, handsome, economical, well-bulit, or durable? Isn't a good book really entertaining, instructive, amusing, funny, engrossing, exciting, beautiful, stirring, stimluating, or well-written?

(b) When you say that a teacher is "good," what do you really mean? Precisely what thought is in your mind? Do you mean that the teacher is patient, intelligent, kind, well-informed, expert, skillful, helpful, or firm?

(c) Think of all the words that you might properly use to describe a "good" moving-picture, a "good" baseball game, a "good" dinner, and a "good" party.

(d) There are many slangy ways to convey the idea of "good"; these you should avoid. You had better say "good" rather than use such words as *great*, *swell*, *peachy*, *wonderful*, and *glorious*, when all you mean by such words is an expression of general approval. Such words are probably permissible when you are speaking very informally, but not when you are trying to use acceptable English and certainly not when you are making a particular attempt to increase and stimulate your vocabulary.

Section 19 discusses the misuse of another over-worked word, *bad*.

10

Can You Answer These Questions?

a) Why is it that none of your friends is ambitious to be a *culprit*?

(b) Why is the *crisis* of a war a particularly important time?

(c) What similarity is there between a tennis racket and a *lute*?

(d) Is *marrow* usually found inside boxes, trees, bones, books, telephone poles, or seaweed?

(e) How many rulers are usually at the head of a *monarchy*?

(f) What happens when someone *divulges* a secret? Does he continue to keep it secret, or does he reveal it?

(g) What would happen to a train if the two rails on which it is running were to *diverge*?

(h) Why would you refuse to buy a dog that has *rabies*?

(i) Why should members of a *legislature* be *scrupulous*?

Section 15 has more questions like the ones in this section.

11

Families of Words

Here are more words which reveal themselves at a glance as being members of families. You will probably know the first word in each group; if others in a group are unfamiliar, look them up in a dictionary. Then use each word in a sentence.

(a) receive, reception, receptacle, receptive

(b) vocal, vocation, vocabulary, vociferous

(c) vital, vitality, vitamin, vitals

(d) respond, response, responsible, responsive

(e) nature, naturalist, naturalize, naturally

The next section that deals with Families of Words is Section 21.

12

Ten Words from *Tales from Shakespeare*, by Charles and Mary Lamb

Rewrite the following sentences, changing the meaning and wording as little as possible but substituting synonyms for the italicized words. Be sure you know the meaning of the italicized word before you undertake to change it.

1. Antonio, with tears and sad words of sorrow and *repentance*, *implored* his brother's forgiveness; and the king expressed his sincere *remorse* for having assisted Antonio to *depose* his brother.

2. Lysander was in great *affliction* at hearing these evil *tidings*.

3. Puck, to make *amends* for his former mistake, had *contrived* with the utmost *diligence* to bring them all to the same spot, unknown to each other; and he had carefully removed the charm from off the eyes of Lysander with the *antidote* the fairy king gave to him.

13
Synonyms

In Section 3 we gave some attention to synonyms, those groups of words, like *big, large, huge,* and *enormous,* that are close to each other in meaning. Sometimes we can gather as many as twenty or thirty words that are synonymous.

One interesting fact about synonyms, however, is that though any two of them may be almost identical in meaning, their meanings are never precisely the same. If synonyms had exactly the same meaning, our language would be cluttered up with many useless words. As it is, every word is useful to us because each word is the *only* word that carries its precise meaning.

No matter, then, how close in meaning two words may appear at first glance, they really have important and useful differences. Both an enormous house and a big house are large, but obviously an enormous house is larger than one which is merely large. A beautiful picture is more beautiful than a pretty picture, and a tiny child is smaller than a little child. So it is with all synonyms *beautiful* and *pretty, tiny* and *little*; one of the words will have more power and force than its synonym, or will be used somewhat differently.

The Growing Vocabulary

Let us consider some more pairs of synonyms and examine their differences. *Old* and *ancient*, for example, are synonyms, but one of them would serve better than the other to describe a Greek temple built twenty-five hundred years ago. Which is it?

(a) Similarly, *frightened* and *terrified* are synonyms. Which man is more afraid, one who is frightened or one who is terrified?

(b) *Careful* and *cautious*: which word suggests more caution than the other ?

(c) Would you rather carry a *heavy* burden or a *ponderous* burden? Why?

(d) What is the difference in meaning between *strong* and *powerful*? Which adjective would be more appropriate to describe an elephant?

(e) Who tries harder, a person who *strives* to succeed, or one who *tries* to succeed?

(f) Would you rather have a friend who is *curious* about your private affairs, or one who is *inquisitive*? Explain why.

(g) If you invite some friend to go on a picnic with you, would you rather have him *willing* to go, or *eager* to go? Why?

The next section dealing with synonyms is Section 23.

14
Definitions

Explain in your own words what each of the following words means. Imagine that you are talking to someone who does not understand the word at all and make perfectly clear to him just what you mean when you use the word:

recipe	witch	cloud
sleep	apple	ink
table	eraser	sleeve
tax	pencil	garage
oar	exercise	chimney

Section 24 also deals with Definitions.

15

Can You Answer These Questions?

(a) Why should we eat *nutritious* food?

(b) Why is a huge rock not ordinarily used as a *missle*?

(c) Why is none of your classmates likely to be a national *celebrity* for some years?

(d) Why would most people rather send an *invoice* than receive one?

(e) Is your *jugular* vein in your arm, your neck, your foot, or your heart?

(f) How should you like to be a *paragon*? Why?

(g) Why are the deepest parts of the ocean sometimes call *fathomless*?

(h) What happens when a person is *indicted*? How do you pronounce the word?

(i) Why is it impossible for a person to become a *pentagon*?

(j) Why is travel by automobile considered as one kind of *locomotion*?

There are more questions like these in Section 20.

16

Ten Words from *Treasure Island* by Robert Louis Stevenson

The vocabulary of *Treasure Island* is not difficult, probably because Stevenson wrote the book especially for boys, not for adults. There are, however, a good many words in the book which you may not know

Substitute a synonym for each of the italicized words. Do you think that Stevenson used the best word in each case, or is your substitute an improvement? Why?

Altogether I paid pretty dear for my monthly fourpenny piece, in the shape of these *abominable* fancies.

I'm a *magistrate*; and if I catch a breath of complaint against you, if it's only for a piece of *incivility* like tonight's, I'll take *effectual* means to have you hunted down and *routed* out of this. Let that *suffice*.

I'll give you a golden guinea for a *noggin*.

The hamlet lay on the other side of the next *cove*.

Under the clothes the *miscellany* began.

Overcoming a strong *repugnance*, I tore open his shirt at the neck.

17

How Many Do You Know?

Here is another pair of lists, like that in Section 7. In the second column you will find a synonym for each word in the first column. Match them, and on a separate sheet of paper write the synonyms in pairs, as you did in Section 7.

bandit	frankness
contentment	substitute ruler
frenzy	excitement
ally	crowning
allusion	beauty
coronation	unbeliever
lute	boulevard
regent	vastness
infidel	stringed musical instrument
immensity	narrow street
	robber
	finger
	indirect reference
	associate
	eagle
	happiness

Section 27 is the next section like this one.

18

Imitative Words

If you are interested in Imitative Words (See Section 8), you will find one of Poe's poems, *The Bells*, particularly interesting. Here are some lines from that poem which contain words imitative of sounds of various kinds of bells. Write a list of these imitative words.

> Hear the loud alarum bells,
>> Brazen bells!
> What a tale of terror, now, their turbulency tells!
>> In the startled air of night
>> How they scream out their affright!
>> Too much horrified to speak,
>> They can only shriek, shriek,
>>> Out of tune,
> In a clamorous appeal to the mercy of the fire.
>
>> How they clang, and clash, and roar!
>> What a horror they outpour
> On the bosom of the palpitating air!
>> Yet the ear it fully knows,
>>> By the twanging
>>> And the clanging,

How the danger ebbs and flows:
Yet the ear distinctly tells,
    In the jangling
    And the wrangling.
How the danger sinks and swells.

Another poet who particularly loved to use words imitative of sounds was Tennyson. Here are a few of his verses; from them select the imitative words. In each case decide what Tennyson was attempting to imitate:

Myriads of rivulets hurrying through the lawn,
The moan of doves in immemorial elms
And murmuring of innumerable bees.
I do but sing because I must,
And pipe but as the linnets sing.

Calm is the morn without a sound,
    Calm as to suit a calmer grief,
And only through the faded leaf
    The chestnut pattering to the ground.

Dry clashed his harness in the icy caves
And barren chasms, and all to left and right
The bare black cliff clanged round him, as he based
His feet on juts of slippery crag that rang
Sharp-smitten with the dint of armed heels.

Section 28 continues the discussion of Imitative Words.

19

Bad

In Section 9 it was pointed out that the word *good* is overworked. Whenever people want to express approval of anything at all, they are likely to use the word *good*, though there are hundreds of other words that would more accurately express the meaning that they wish to convey.

Similarly, when people want to express disapproval or dislike of something, they are liable to use the word *bad*, though there are hundreds of other words which, in special circumstances, would serve them better to express their idea. Just as there was nothing "wrong" with the word *good*, so there is nothing wrong with *bad*; but it is lazy and rather stupid to use the same word over and over again, without discrimination, when with a little trouble we can find a word that means what we really want to say. You will find people who drive to church on a bad day and listen to a bad sermon and on the way home see a bad accident at a bad corner or perhaps get a bad headache. Wouldn't it be preferable to call the sermon dull or boring, to describe the accident as serious or fatal, to call the day rainy, wet, wintry, or stormy, and to describe the corner as dangerous, depending in each case upon what one really means?

Here are some sentences containing the word *bad*. In each case a more suitable word can be found. Write the sentences, substituting for *bad* a word which more accurately indicates just what you mean to say; select your word from the list below:

(a) He had a bad time at school because he was so bad in his studies and because his behavior was so bad.

(b) There is a bad hill near my house with a bad curve at the bottom on which many bad accidents have occurred.

(c) He was such a bad sailor that I feared he would overturn his sailboat in a bad storm.

unhappy	poor	weak	great	unsuccessful
unskillful	serious	sharp	disobedient	backward
unfortunate	steep	blind	clumsy	dangerous
discourteous	heavy	reckless	furious	fatal

Section 29 discusses the use and the avoidance of another overworked word, *very*.

20

More Questions

(a) Why is Germany not considered a *democracy*?

(b) Does a clergyman wear a *surplice*, a *surplus*, or both?

(c) Why do mot people hope that their handwriting is *legible*?

(d) If you were ill, why would you seek the help of a *physician* rather than an *attorney*?

(e) In what months is snow *exceptional*?

(f) What is George Washington's *surname*?

(g) How can a disease and a laugh both properly be called *infectious*?

(h) Why is it that when you blow upon a *cornea*, it does not make a sound like a cornet?

(i) Why is it usually less dangerous to stand on a *binnacle* than on a pinnacle?

More questions may be found in Section 30.

21

Families of Words

Here are five more families of words. As in Sections 1 and 11, you will probably know the first word of each family, but you may not know all the others. When you come upon an unfamiliar word, look it up in your dictionary and write the word in a sentence. You should write at least five sentences, one for each family.

(a) annual, annuity, annals

(b) error, err, erratic, errant

(c) question, quest, questionable, query, questionnaire

(d) shorten, shortage, shortsighted, shorthand, shorthanded, shortstop, shortening

(e) profit, profitable, unprofitable, profiteer.

The next section that concerns itself with word-families is Section 31, in Part II of this book. It is harder than Sections 1, 11, and 21.

22

Ten Words from *Kidnapped*, by Robert Louis Stevenson

Explain what each of the following sentences means, being sure that you understand the meanings of the italicized words:

"Ye have some *rudiments* of sense," said Alan grimly.

The roads were *infested* with beggars.

The chief singer in our boat struck into a *melancholy* air.

The more *indistinct* the *accusations* were, the less I liked them, for they left the wider field to *fancy*.

The woman's face lit up with a *malignant* anger.

The time passed so lightly in this good company, that I began to be almost *reconciled* to my residence at Shaws.

I looked at that ship with an extreme *abhorrence*.

It should be his part to find a ship and to arrange for Alan's safe *embarkation*.

23

Synonyms

In Sections 3 and 13 we studied synonyms, those groups of words like *little*, *small*, *tiny*, and *minute* that have similar meaning, though never precisely the same one.

In the left-hand column below are five words. Take each of them one by one and in the right-hand column find four words that are synonymous. When you are looking for the synonyms of *church*, for example, you will at once see in the right-hand column the word *temple*; and as you look down a little farther, you will come upon *chapel*. *Temple* and *chapel* are two of the four synonyms for which you are looking. What are the other two?

church	temple
	recompense
	knave
	sorcery
witchcraft	rogue
	renumeration
	magic
	chapel
ghost	specter
	mosque
	phantom

	indemnity
	synagogue
	compensation
reward	witchery
	apparition
	rascal
	spirit
villain	blackguard
	hero
	enchantment
	palace

The next section dealing with Synonyms is Section 33.

24

Definitions

(a) Some years ago, when radios were still novelties and when people living far from cities and towns had not yet installed radio-receivers, a city man hunting in the backwoods of Maine encountered a trapper who lived there all the year round, fifty miles from the nearest small village.

> "You must get bored and lonely," remarked the vistor from the city. "Why don't you buy yourself a radio?" he asked.

> The trapper looked inquiringly at the other.

> "What is a radio?" he asked.

> "It's a sort of thing you can hear speeches and music through."

> "Oh," said the trapper, understanding lighting his face, "you mean an ear-trumpet?"

> "No, no. I mean an electrical machine that plays music and things like that."

> "You don't mean a phonograph, maybe?" asked the trapper.

It was five minutes before the city visitor succeeded in making the trapper understand. What would you have told the trapper when he asked, "What is a radio?"

(b) Imagine that you have just met someone who has never seen a fog or even heard of one. How would you explain fog to him in such a way that he would not confuse it with rain, smoke, steam, or dust clouds?

(c) What is a chair? Try to make a statement that will not make one think that a bench, a stool, a window-seat, or a table is also a chair.

(d) "A necktie is something worn around the neck for decoration." What do you think of that as a clear definition? If that is an accurate definition of a necktie, then a necklace must be a necktie, too, for it is "something worn around the neck for decoration." Try to make a definition of a necktie which will prevent anyone from thinking that a collar, a fur, or a necklace is likewise a necktie.

25

Vocabulary Test on Part One.
How Many Do You Know?

Below are twenty-five short sentences or phrases, each containing an italicized word derived from Sections 1 to 24. Each sentence or phrase is followed by five words, one of which is a synonym of the italicized word. Find that one of the five words which you think closest in meaning to the italicized word.

Sentence Number 0 is an example. The problem here is to find a synonym for the italicized word, *tall*. The word you are looking for is the third of the five words, *high*. Indicate your answer by writing on a separate sheet of paper "0-high." Similarly in Sentence 1, if you think *persuasive* means "clear," write "1-clear."

0. A *tall* buliding:
   white, old, high, thin, famous

1. A *persuasive* argument:
   clear, convincing, interesting, dull, funny

2. A *perpetual* mystery:
   exciting, occasional, eternal, deep, national

3. Farming is his *vocation*:
   hope, detestation, downfall, occuption, hobby

4. She received an *annuity*:
   yearly payment, injury, ring, insult, volume

5. The meeting *adjourned*:
   began, ended, voted, elected officers,
   passed resolutions

6. An elephant's *proboscis*:
   foot, eye, tooth, trunk, leg

7. An *obstinate* girl:
   pretty, well-dressed, stupid, happy, stubborn

8. He carried a *portmanteau*:
   radio, traveling-bag, small book, cane,
   fishing rod

9. *Abominable* ideas:
   brilliant, hateful, old-fashioned, artistic, clever

10. *Civil* language:
    foreign, unpleasant, slangy, polite, boastful

11. A *melancholy* song:
    sad, gay, rapid, funny, tuneful

12. He is a *knave*:
    boy, athlete, villain, priest, lawyer

13. We saw a *specter*:
    pair of eyeglasses, speck, sky-scraper,
    policeman, ghost.

14. *Odious* behavior:
    virtuous, wicked, natural, detestable, amusing

15. An *alert* sentry:
    watchful, sleepy, angry, hostile, friendly

16. An *invoice* came in the package:
    radio, premium, lamp, record, bill

17. A good *attorney*:
    ball-player, storyteller, driver, doctor,
    lawyer

18. He was *apprehensive*:
    strong, handsome, fearful, happy,
    discourteous

19. *Vociferous* children:
    thin, ill-nourished, timid, clamorous, sickly

20. A peculiar *query*:
    man, jest, appearance, question, offer

21. The *rudiments* of learning:
    fundamentals, pleasures, pains, purposes,
    teachers

22. A *unified* nation:
    foreign, military, united, enormous,
    democratic

23. *Synonymous* words:
    similar, large, eloquent, pious, literary

24. A *malignant* sneer:
    quick, sad, malicious, cheerful, thoughtful

25. She worked *diligently*:
    slowly, industriously, gaily, clumsily, sullenly

A key to this test will be found on page 178.

The
Growing
Vocabulary

Fun and Adventure with Words

Part Two

26

Ten words from *The Pied Piper of Hamelin*, by Robert Browning

The following lines from *The Pied Piper* are particularly easy to memorize. If you will learn these lines by heart, you will find it easier to remember the unfamiliar words.

Write a sentence using each of the italicized words (ten sentences altogether).

Be sure you know the meaning of the word before you attempt to use it.

To see the townsfolk suffer so
From *vermin*, was a pity.

They ate the cheese out of the *vats*.

At this the mayor and *corporation*
Quaked with a mighty *consternation*.

Insulted by a lazy *ribald*
With idle pipe and *vesture piebald*

In Transylvania there's a tribe
Of *alien* people who *ascribe*

The outlandish ways and dress
On which their neighbors lay such stress
To their fathers and mothers having risen
Out of some *subterraneous* prison.

What is a *pied* piper?

27

How Many Do You Know?

In the second column find a synonym for each word in the first column. Write the pairs of synonyms as you did in Section 7.

fraudulent	dishonest
slothful	flexible
dumfounded	filthy
pliable	greedy
squalid	lazy
pecuniary	ridiculous
avaricious	prudent
maroon	astounded
mongrel	financial
precipitous	of mixed breed
	depressing
	dark red
	hopeful
	truthful
	glorious
	very steep

Section 37 is the next exercise in matching synonyms.

28

Imitative Words

The imitative words discussed in Sections 8 and 18 are imitative of sounds. There is another kind of imitative word, not so common, which imitates, or at least gives an impression of, the very thing which it signifies. Such a word is *zigzag*, whose two z's are themselves zigzags; the word *zigzag* is much more closely imitative of the appearance and feeling of a zigzag than is, for instance, the word *level*.

Here are some other words imitative of appearances and giving a sensation that corresponds fairly closely to the meaning of the word. It is not always easy to explain, however, just why the word sounds or looks like what it means.

> wriggle (write the word and notice how the w
> and the g's wriggle)

sparkle	gloom
glitter	scramble
sprinkle	scurry
slither	level
skim (verb)	

(a) Use each of the above words in an appropriate sentence.

(b) What other words can you think of that sound or look like what they mean? Avoid words that imitate sounds, like *murmur*, *purr*, and *scream*. That kind of word was dealt with in Sections 8 and 18.

29
Very

Everyone has in his vocabulary a great many words which he seldom remembers to use. An effective way to remind yourself to put into action some of your most useful adjectives is to stop when you find yourself about to say or write such phrases as "very big," "very old," or "very happy." Instead of using *very* and a common, overworked adjective, find a single word which by itself means "very big," (such as *enormous*), "very old" (such as *aged* or *ancient*), and "very happy" (such as *joyful, joyous,* or *blissful*).

Rewrite the following sentences, substituting for the two italicized words a single word that has the same meaning:

(a) One of the brothers is industrious, but the other is *very lazy.*

(b) Small children are often *very afraid* in the dark.

(c) If a person had no money at all, he is *very poor.*

(d) The bumpers of the new automobile were *very bright.*

(e) The actions of the clown were *very funny*.

(f) The hill was *very steep*.

(g) The weather today is *very cold*.

(h) After his fortieth birthday he grew *very fat*.

(i) He was always *very hopeful*.

(j) The room was *very dirty*.

Section 39 deals with two much overworked words, *go* and its past tense *went*.

30

Can You Answer These Questions?

(a) Why would you avoid tying a package with a hawser?

(b) Would you feel flattered if someone said that your literary style is *pellucid*? Why, or why not?

(c) Is a *preachment* much the same thing as a sermon?

(d) Why is it that even boiling a *hogshead* will not make it *edible*?

(e) Why can't you reach the *zenith* as long as your feet are on the ground?

(f) Why is it generally undesirable to *yaw* in a boat race?

(g) When you have learned something by *rote*, does that mean that you have learned it by writing it down, by heart, or by doing it?

(h) In general, why do people object to high *tariffs*?

(i) Is it true that a *stoat* is the same animal as a weasel?

More questions to be answered will be found in Section 40.

31

Families of Words

Here are some more families of words that resemble each other in appearance and are related to each other in meaning.

Examine these families with care. When you come upon a word whose meaning you do not know or about which you are doubtful, look the word up in a dictionary and then write it into a sentence of your own.

(a) myth, mythological, mythical, mythology
(b) merit, merited, meritorious
(c) prospect, prospective, prospector, prospectus
(d) stupid, stupidity, stupefy, stupefaction
(e) hypocrite, hypocrisy, hypocritical
(f) percipice, precipitate, precipitous, precipitation, precipitant

If you enjoy making the acquaintance of unfamiliar members of word-families, turn to Section 41 before reading any other sections in this book. Don't forget, however, that the real secret of learning new words is to read about them in a sizeable dictionary and to use them as soon as possible in speech or in writing.

32

Fifteen Words from
The Sketch Book, by Washington Irving

Rewrite the following sentences, substituting a word or phrase of your own for each of the italicized words. Be sure in making your substitutions not to change the meaning of the sentence.

Those men are most apt to be *obsequious* and *conciliating* abroad who are under the discipline of *shrews* at home.

The great error in Rip's composition was an *insuperable aversion* to all kinds of profitable labor.

I have often wondered at the extreme *fecundity* of the press, and how it comes to pass that so many heads, on which Nature seems to have inflicted the curse of barrenness, yet teem with *voluminous* productions.

Her aunts, having been great flirts and *coquettes* in their younger days, were admirably calculated to be *vigilant* guardians and strict *censors* of the conduct of their niece; for there is no *duenna* so rigidly *prudent*, and *inexorably decorous*, as a *superannuated* coquette.

33
Synonyms

Here are ten sentences, each containing an italicized word. Rewrite the sentences, supplying a synonym in place of each italicized word. In so doing, keep the original meaning of the sentence.

After the sentences you will find a list of words containing the synonyms that you need.

(a) He was so *obese* that he could not rise to his feet with ease.

(b) With her skill in painting, she had an *incalculable* advantage over other girls.

(c) Most people *loathe* snakes.

(d) The loyalty of a dog is a *consolation* in time of trouble.

(e) The detective climbed the *circular* staircase.

(f) He was *incensed* by detective's remark.

(g) The *desertion* of a friend in trouble is inexcusable.

(h) After a hard day's work, one naturally seeks *repose*.

(i) I could find no means of *persuading* him to sell his books.

(j) She is an *able* teacher in arithmetic.

exaggerated	displeased	injured
fat	burden	round
old	slanting	love
inestimable	true	dangerous
hate	kill	rest
laugh at	angered	new
comfort	amused	inducing
smart	abandonment	amusement
forcing	competent	cheerful

If you enjoy finding synonyms, you might go at once to Section 43.

34

True or False?

Here are ten statements involving a knowledge of the meanings of words. If you think a statement is true, mark it **T**; if false, mark it **F**.

To score your results, add the number of correct answers and subtract from the total the number of wrong answers. For example, if you have 7 correct answers and 3 wrong ones, your final score would be 4 (7 − 3 = 4)

When you find a word that you do not know, learn its meaning and try to use it soon either in your speech or your writing.

1. A timorous man is often fearful

2. Larceny is much the same as theft.

3. A spiral is egg-shaped.

4. Epilepsy is gross dishonesty.

5. A manifesto is a declaration or proclamation.

6. All prismatic colors are either red or yellow.

7. Imbecility is an undesirable state of mind.

8. When one delivers a speech, it is well to try to speak balderdash.

9. Crass ingorance is worse than mere ingorance.

10. *Guerrilla* is just another way to spell *gorilla*.

Section 44 contains more sentences to be marked true or false.

35

Verbs and Nouns

Most verbs have nouns which correspond to them. *Glorify* and *glory,* *open* and *opening,* *happen* and *happening,* *cultivate* and *cultivation* are examples of corresponding verbs and nouns.

The corresponding noun does not always resemble its verb so closely as in the examples above. The noun which corresponds to *suspect,* for instance, is *suspicion; recognition* corresponds to *recognize;* and *sight* corresponds to the verb *see.*

Here are a dozen verbs; find the noun which corresponds to each, and use each of the nouns in a sentence of your own making.

seclude	perturb
convert	presume
impeach	pretend
misconceive	recite
observe	decide
perplex	reprehend

Don't guess! Use a dictionary.

The next section similar to this is Section 45, which deals with corresponding nouns and adjectives.

36

Fifteen Words from
Silas Marner, by George Eliot

Explain the meaning of each of the following sentences. The hardest words are italicized; be sure you know their meanings before you try to tell the meaning of the sentences as a whole.

1. There might be seen, in districts far away among the lanes, or deep in the bosoms of the hills, certain *pallid*, undersized men, who, by the side of the *brawny* country-folk, looked like the *remnants* of a *disinherited* race.

2. He was believed to be a young man of *exemplary* life and *ardent* faith; and a peculiar interest had been centered in him ever since he had fallen, at a prayer-meeting, into a mysterious *rigidity* and *suspension* of consciousness.

3. The results of confession were not *contingent*, they were certain; whereas betrayal was not certain. From the near vision of that certainty he fell back on suspense and *vacillation* with a sense of repose.

4. He felt that in letting Dunstan have the money he had already been guilty of a *breach* of trust hardly less *culpable* than that of spending the money directly for his own *behoof.*

5. Like many violent and *implacable* men, he allowed evils to grow under favor of his own heedlessness, till they pressed upon him with exasperating force, and then he turned round with fierce severity and became *unrelentingly* hard.

37

How Many Do You Know?

This section is like Section 27. In the second column below find a synonym for each word in the first column. Write the pairs of synonyms on a sheet of paper.

boulder	lawmaker
legislator	flavor
globule	hat
pinafore	senate
savor	large rock
jaunt	safety pin
glutton	greedy eater
incumbrance	income
nucleus	small sphere
rendezvous	meeting place
	short trip
	apron
	hope
	burden
	shooting star
	something new
	central part
	happiness

Section 47 is the next section like this one.

38

Latin

Until comparatively recently Latin was the language by which learned men of different nationalities and races, as well as the leaders of the Roman Catholic Church, communicated with each other. It was in Latin, too, that scholarly books were written, as, for example, Sir Isaac Newton's famous work, the *Principia Mathematica*, published in 1687.

These reasons for learning Latin have largely disappeared, but some knowledge of Latin is still most vaulable for the thorough understanding of the meanings of thousands of words in the English language. The particular purpose of the Latin sections of this book (Sections 38, 48, 58, 68, and 78) is to give those who have studied no Latin at all a greater command over some of the words which we owe to the Romans. Others, who know something of Latin, will find many words with which they are familiar appearing, perhaps, in unfamiliar guise.

(Incidentally, referring to the last sentence you have read, one is naturally "familiar" with anything that is found in one's own "*familia*," the Latin word for "family" or "household.")

Here are some common examples of how a

knowledge of Latin words leads to an increased knowledge of English words:

> From the Latin word *spectare* (meaning "to look at") come *spectacles, spectacle, spectator, prospect, specter, spectrum, spectacular,* and *expect*. If you do not know what a spectacle is, look up the word. Do the same with *spectrum* and *specter*.

> From *portare*, meaning "to carry," come the English words *porter, transport, import, export, support, deportment, portfolio, portable, portage, portmanteau*. What have *portage* and *protmanteau* to do with the idea of "to carry"?

> From *audire*, meaning "to hear," we have *audience, audible, auditory, audition, auditor,* and *auditorium*. What are the auditory nerves? What is an inaudible sound? What is a radio audition? And what is an auditor at a lecture?

> From *errare*, a Latin word meaning "to wander," come *erratic, error, erroneous, err,* and *knight-errant*. What is a knight-errant? What happens when a person errs?

If you will make a careful study of these groups of words, you will find that the fundamental meaning of the Latin word occurs in each of the English words derived from it.

Section 48 continues the dicussion of English words derived from Latin.

39

Go and *Went*

Go, and its past tense *went*, are overworked words like *good* (Section 9), *bad* (Section 19), and *very* (Section 29). It is often easy to find a more vigorous or expressive word to suit your purpose, especially when *go* and *went* are used in the sense of *travel* (*ed*).

The turtle went slowly along the sidewalk.

The boy went whistling down the street.

The runner went one hundred yards in ten seconds.

The automobile went rapidily down the road.

The airplane went rapidly across the sky.

Above are five sentences, all containing the word *went*. Five different speeds of travel are suggested, however; surely it is possible to find five different verbs which will more accurately suggest the speed of travel than *went* does. Wouldn't it be an improvement to say, for instance,

The turtle crept along the sidewalk.

The Growing Vocabulary: Part Two

The boy strode whistling down the street.

The runner sprinted one hundred yards in ten seconds.

The automobile dashed down the road.

The airplane sped across the sky.

Here is a list of words which can often be advantageously substituted for *go* and *went*:

speed	post	scuttle	scurry	whiz	whisk
hasten	fly	race	shoot	tear	limp
spurt	stream	plod	trudge	flit	totter
sprint	sweep	skim	move	slide	dart
crawl	saunter	rush	dash	spring	stagger
walk	march	drag	pass	glide	scamper
trail	ride	hurry	creep	step	toddle
loiter	lag	inch	steal	jog	meander
lumber	roll	drift	run	wander	coast
flow	travel	journey	migrate	roam	
stride	pace	tramp	stalk	strut	
float	cruis	voyage	emigrate	struggle	along

The words in the list above are purposely arranged in no particular order. Write answers to the following questions:

(a) From the list slect five words that mean "go fast"; use each in a sentence.

(b) Find five words that mean "go slowly," and use each in a sentence.

(c) What five words suggest travel on foot?

(d) What one word denotes the slowest motion?

(e) What one word suggests the fastest motion?

(f) What words are particularly applicable to the motion of water or air?

(g) What words imply weakness, or travel with a burden?

(h) What words are used particularly in connection with travel on water?

Section 49 deals with another overworked word, *thing*.

40

More Questions

Answer the following questions. Do not guess at the meanings of unfamilar of doubtful words; look them up in a dictonary. If your answer is "yes" or "no", give your reason for it.

(a) Is it true that people are usally debiliatated by rest and good food?

(b) Which of the following is properly described by the adjective *livid*: the red face of an angry person, blood, grass, a dull-bluish bruise, or brightly colored sunset?

(c) Why is it that though most people want to make money, they do not want to make spurious money?

(d) Do you consider docility a desirable quality in a dog?

(e) Is it true that a languorous athelete is almost sure to distinguish himself by his athletic achievements?

(f) Why is it that one cannot make a rebus without drawing pictures?

(g) Why you have never had obsequies to celebrate your birthday?

(h) What is the antonym of *convexity*?

(i) Do you consider it desirable to have a furtive manner?

(j) Many king and princes possess mausoleums. Should you like to live in one? Why?

You will find more questions like these in Section 55.

41
Families of Words

Here are six more families of words. If you know one word in a family, you will find that the others become a part of your vocablulary more quickly than they otherwise might.

Use at least two words from each family in sentences of your own. Write twelve sentences altogether.

(a) orator, oration, oral, oratory, oracle, oratorio

(b) remit, remittance, remission, remiss, remissness

(c) ferocious, ferocity

(d) audience, audible, auditorium, auditor, audition, auditory (See Section 38)

(e) defense, defenseless, defensible, defensive

(f) measure, measurement, measurable, measured, measureless

The next section that deals with Families of Words is Section 81.

42

Fifteen More Words from *Tales from Shakespeare*, By Charles and Mary Lamb

Explain in your own words the meaning of each of the following sentences, taking special pains to make clear the meanings of the italicized words:

1. How far he was right in this *conjecture*, and what he ought to think of his mother, how far she was *privy* to this murder, and whether by her consent or knowledge, or without, it came to pass, were the doubts which continually *harassed* and *distracted* him.

2. Malcom took upon himself the government, which, by the *machinations* of the *usurper*, he had so long been deprived of, and ascended the throne among the *acclamations* of the nobles and the people.

3. He shut himself up in his castle, whose *impregnable* strength was such as defied a seige.

4. She knew him to be ambitious, but withal to be *scrupulous*, and not yet

prepared for that height of crime which commonly in the end accompanies *inordinate* ambitition.

5. He was a *usurer*, who had *amassed* an immense fortune.

6. It was soon agreed that, as Demetrius had given up his *pretensions* to Hermia, he should endeavor to *prevail upon* her father to *revoke* the cruel sentence of death.

43
Synonyms

Here are ten more sentences, like those in Section 33, each of which contains an italicized word. Rewrite each sentence, substituting a synonym for the italicized word. The synonym that you want can be found somewhere in the list of words following the sentences.

(a) He lives his life in complete *felicity*.

(b) The sky was *void* of clouds.

(c) She was *dexterous* in her sewing.

(d) They sat in a *semicircle*.

(e) His adventures are *unbelievable*.

(f) This hill is the *habitation* of foxes.

(g) The sailors *forsook* the ship.

(h) We spent three days in the *dungeon*.

(i) They had fifteen minutes of *animated* conversation.

(j) Do you like books about *buccaneers*?

fascinating	old church	bucking horses	living place
full	half circle	incredible	hunting ground
full circle	truthful	eating place	burial place
empty	skillful	poverty	rigged
clumsy	misery	funny	saluted
circus	happy	abandoned	forest
prison cell	boat	happiness	lively
adventures	anger	insulting	pirates

Sections 53, 63, 73, and 83 deal with antonyms, words that are just the opposite of synonyms. You may want to turn at once to Section 53.

44

True or False?

Here are ten more sentences like those in Section 34; they are to be marked either T or F, indicating that you think the statement true or false. Write your answers on separate paper, and give your reason for your opinon.

1. Apes are famous for their superlative beauty.
2. An optimistic person usually feels discouraged.
3. A boxer is said to be convalescent just before a fight.
4. A coot is an insect.
5. Incensed sometimes means "angry."
6. Garrulous means "stationary."
7. It is impolite to be voracious at the table.
8. A knoll is a small hill.
9. A harpsichord is a kind of piano.
10. Indelible ink cannot be erased.

Section 54 contains more sentences to be marked true or false.

45

Nouns and Adjectives

Many nouns have adjectives which correspond. *Arithmetic* and *arithmetical, heaven* and *heavenly, name* and *nominal, adjective* and *adjectival, observance* and *observant, prevalence* and *prevalent,* and *repetition* and *repetitious* are examples.

What adjectives correspond to the following nouns? Use each adjective in a sentence of your own, being sure first of all that you know the exact meaning of the adjective. Don't guess!

deception	period
scandal	municipality
book	profit
improbability	profundity
moment	reception
enigma	revolution
nucleus	simplicity

Section 85 deals with adjectives and their corresponding nouns.

46

Fifteen Words from *The Last of the Mohicans*, by James Fenimore Cooper

Do as you did in Section 32. Rewrite the sentences, substituting a word or phrase of your own for each of the italicized words.

1. *Emulating* the patience and self-denial of the practised native warriors, they learned to overcome every difficulty.

2. The forts were taken and retaken, *razed* and rebuilt.

3. There was no ear so deaf as not to have drunk in with *avidity* the narrative of some fearful tale of midnight slaughter.

4. This *abstinence*, when he possessed the means of satisfying hunger, at length attracted the notice of Heyward.

5. The *environs* of the fort were filled with violence and uproar.

6. The verdure of the plain looked as though it were *scathed* by the consuming lightning.

7. The whole landscape appeared now like

some pictured *allegory* of life.

8. His blood curdled when he found himself in absolute contact with such fierce and *implacable* enemies.

9. The other Indian bowed his head, as if *palsied* by terror or stricken with shame.

10. The *artifice* was answered by a hundred voices raised in *imprecations*.

11. Nothing could be distinguished but a dark mass of human forms tossed and involved in *inexplicable* confusion.

12. The woman placed her arms *akimbo*.

13. A youngster attempted to assist the *termagant*.

14. This solemn pause was known by all present to be the grave *precursor* of a weighty and important judgement.

47

How Many Do You Know?

Match the words in the first column with their synonyms in the second column.

to foreknow	to plunder
to incite	to see into something
to maraud	to make candy
to particularize	to act like a villain
to reminisce	to stir up
to segregate	to profane
to snivel	to filter or sift
to vilify	to whine; to whimper
to desecrate	to mention individually
to flinch	to know ahead of time
to perforate	to shrink from
	to become a minister
	to set apart from others
	to make holes in
	to recall past happenings
	to be peculiar
	to speak evil of

Use each of the words in the first column in a sentence of your own.

The next section in which there is a chance to match synonyms is Section 57.

48
Latin

Certain common Latin words, as we have seen in Section 38, have many descendants or derivatives in English. A knowledge of the Latin makes the connection between the derivatives clear.

Here are some groups of words in which all the members are related in meaning and form to the parent Latin word.

From the Latin *tangere*, meaning "to touch" we get *tangible, intangible, tangent, contact, intact*, and *contiguous*. The last three, at first glance, do not seem related to *tangere*; they come, however, from another form of that word.

(a) What is a tangent to a circle and why is it so called?

(b) What country is contiguous to the United States? Why?

(c) Name one object that is tangible. Name somthing that is intangible.

From *habitare*, "to dwell," come *inhabitant, habitation, habitable*, and *habitat*.

(d) Is a house a habitat or a habitation?

(e) What are the normal inhabitants of habitats?

The Latin word *currere* means "to run"; from it we get our English words *current* (two meanings), *occur*, *recurrent*, *curriculum*, *currency*, and *courier*.

(f) What kind of applause is recurrent?

(g) In what sense does a courier run?

Latin *dormire* means "to sleep"; the English words *dormitory*, *dormant*, and *dormouse* come from it.

(h) What are dormant abilities in a person?

Latin *vocare* means "to call"; in English we have words derived from it: *vocal*, *voice*, *vocabulary*, *vocation*, *invoke*, *revoke*, *vociferous*.

(i) What is the difference between a vocation and an avocation?

(j) How does the idea of "to call" enter into both of these words?

You will notice that each group of words derived from a single Latin word really makes up a family of words (see Sections 1, 11, etc.). If you know any Latin, you might turn to Sections 1, 11, 21, 31 and 41 and see how many of the families of words listed in those sections are derived originally from Latin words.

The next section dealing with Latin and its influence of the English vocabulary is Section 58.

49

Thing

One of the most overworked words in our language is the word *thing*. Usually one can find another word which expresses the meaning more accurately. It is lazy and careless, for instance to say: "Things are improving in this country; factories are making more things, and the thing we can all do to help is to buy more things." The sentence might be improved in serveral ways; for example one might say: "Conditions are improving in this country; factories are making more goods, and we can all help by buying more."

There is nothing "wrong" with the word *thing*, any more than there is with the words *good* (Section 9) and *bad* (section 19). It will help you, however, to put into use many words now dorimant in your vocabulary if for a time you will make a conscious effort to avoid *thing* and search in your mind for a more accurate or expressive word.

Here are a few sentences containing examples of the lazy and careless use of *thing*. Rewrite the sentences, substituting a more exact word for *thing* or avoiding the use of *thing* by rewording the sentence completely but preserving the orginal meaning.

> (a) The funny thing is that although he talks a great deal about how many things he does during the day, he really doesn't do a thing.
>
> (b) It is an interesting thing to compare Hitler and Mussolini and the various things that they do.
>
> (c) The thing that impressed us was how big a thing the *Queen Mary* is.
>
> (d) Put your hat on that thing by the door; then come into this room and we shall talk about the things that interest you most.
>
> (e) The thing a player should try to do when he plays basketball is to put the ball through the baskets that hang on things at each end of the court.
>
> (f) The thing that annoys me most about Bill Smith is his discourtesy.

Section 59 deals with two more words frequently overworked in speech and writing, *say* and *ask*.

50

Vocabulary Test on Part Two.
How Many Do You Know?

This test should be done in the same way as the test in Section 25. See the instructions there.

1. Great *consternation*:
   intelligence, beauty, anger, dismay, truth

2. An *obese* boy:
   young, handsome, obedient, fat, talkative

3. He *loathes* onions:
   peels, buys, sells, raises, hates

4. *Repose* for the body:
   rest, medical care, clothes, hard work,
   cold cream

5. Endless *felicity*:
   belt, speech, fatigue, happiness, friendship

6. A *dexterous* horseman:
   skillful, well-dressed, handsome, clumsy, young

7. *Pliable* material:
   waterproof, thick, expensive, flexible, worn-out

8. A *meritorious* case:
   deserving, famous, notorious, large, well-built

9. A *precipitous* descent:
   noteworthy, foreign, steep, slow, long

10. Arrested for *larceny*:
    bigamy, arson, theft, kidnaping, swearing

11. *Optimistic* remarks:
    gloomy, hopeful, injurious, friendly, clever

12. A *garrulous* woman:
    beautiful, ugly, old, wealthy, talkative

13. *Voracious* appetites:
    greedy, small, artificial, birdlike, satisfied

14. Napoleon stood on a *knoll*:
    cannon, tree trunk, small hill, mountain,
    platform

15. She wore a *pinafore*:
    hat, feather, bodice, apron, hatpin

16. The *nucleus* of a group:
    center, leader, edge, size, outline

17. Mary was *incensed* by the remark:
    interested, angered, amused, depressed,
    made happy

18. Odd *vesture*:
    accent, clothing, language, vest, vulture

19. *Subterraneous* water:
    sweet, fast-flowing, brackish, unwholesome,
    underground

20. Among an *alien* people:
    happy, foreign, poverty-stricken, ancient,
    deceptive

21. *Fraudulent* schemes:
high-minded, simple, dishonest, intellectual,
unsuccessful

22. Heavy *precipitation*:
thunder, lightning, burden, rainfall,
misfortune

23. *Pallid* children:
playful, well-dressed, sunburnt, truthful, pale

24. A *furtive* manner:
childlike, stealthy, polite, charming, weary

25. An *impregnable* position:
steady, unstable, invincible, profitable,
dignified

A key to this test will be found on page 178.

The
Growing
Vocabulary
Fun and Adventure with Words

Part Three

51

Prefixes

A prefix is a syllable (or group of syllables) attached to the beginning of a word and affecting its meaning, *Re-*, for instance, means "back"; when *re-* is attached to the beginning of the common word *call* to make *recall*, the meaning of the word becomes "call back."

There are dozens of prefixes that occur in English words. A few of them occur so often that they are worth memorizing. Here are five common prefixes together with their meanings:

ante-	before
circum-	around
sub-	under
anti-	against
mono-	one, single

What are the meanings of the following words? How does the meaning of the prefix enter into the total meaning of each word?

Write each word in a sentence of your own.

(a) antedate, antecedent, ante meridiem (A.M.), anteroom, antediluvian

(b) circumnavigate, circumference, circumlocution, circumscribe

(c) subway, submarine, subconscious, sublease, submerge, subterranean

(d) antislavery, antiseptic, antisocial, antitoxin

(e) monoplane, monarch, monologue, monocle, monogram, monolith, monomania, monosyllable

Section 61 continues the discussion of prefixes.

52

Fifteen Words from *Twice-Told Tales*, by Nathaniel Hawthorne

Can you find synonymous words or phrases for those of the author which are italicized?

(a) My friend expected to *transmute* slate and marble into silver and gold.

(b) The tombstones are adorned with death's-heads, crossbones, scythes, hour-glasses, and other *lugubrious* emblems of mortality.

(c) These productions were brought across the ocean to commemorate the *defunct* worthies of this lonely isle.

(d) It is an old theme of satire, the falsehood and vanity of monumental *eulogies*.

(e) The quaintness of his remarks gave a *raciness* to his talk.

(f) This was Mr Wigglesworth's standing emblem of *conjugal bereavement*.

(g) When we ridicule the *triteness* of monumental verses, we forget that

Sorrow reads far deeper in them than we can.

(h) A *phantasy* arose in my mind of good Mr. Wigglesworth sitting down to dinner at a broad, flat tombstone, and drinking out of a *lachrymatory* vase, or *sepulchral* urn.

(i) Each elder looked at the two candidates with a most *scrutinizing* gaze.

(j) Father Ephraim had admonished him to seek a successor in his *patriarchal* office.

(k) The *bigoted* and haughty *primate* Laud, Archbishop of Canterbury, controlled the religious affairs of the realm.

53

Antonyms

In Sections 3, 13, 23, 33, and 43 we worked with synonyms, those words that have similar meanings, like *elated, happy, joyous, glad,* and *gay.* There is another kind of word, call an antonym, which is the opposite of a synonym; that is, an antonym is a word that means the contrary of another word. *White* is the antonym of *black,* and *big* is the antonym of *little.*

An effective way to stimulate the growth of your vocabulary is to take a word for consideration and search in your mind for one or more antonyms. If you look for antonyms of *low,* for instance, you will think at once of *high* and *tall,* but you may have to go to a dictionary or confer with someone with a vocabulary larger than yours before you discover *elevated, towering, lofty, exalted,* and *eminent.* All these words have meanings opposite to "low." If one or more of them are not familiar to you, look them up and then make a point of using them in your writing.

Make a list of antonyms for

happy (3)	sensible (2)
stupid (4)	wrong (3)

new (4)   slow (4)
easy (2)   big (4)

The figure in parentheses after each word indicates the number of antonyms you should find without seeking help from the dictionary of from some other person.

The next section that deals with antonyms is Section 63.

54

True or False?

This section is like Sections 34 and 44. On a separate sheet of paper mark the answers T or F.

1. If a man is literate, he cannot read.

2. A sagacious person is shrewd.

3. A gimlet is a tack-extractor.

4. A pleasantry is a good-natured, witty remark.

5. A machination is a kind of machine for plowing.

6. A nostrum is a patent medicine.

7. Almost everyone is eager to become a mendicant.

8. A gesticulation is the same as a gesture.

9. An oblique line forms a perfect curve.

10. A reprobate is a wicked person.

Section 64 is the next section containing sentences to be marked true or false.

55

Can You Answer These Questions?

If your answer is "Yes" or "No", give your reason.

(a) Why is it unuusal to felicitate a person upon his misfortunes?

(b) Is it true that malnutrition is good for every child?

(c) How large is an infinitesimal speck of dust?

(d) If you obviate difficulties, does that mean that you clear them out of the way?

(e) What is the difference between a morion and a moron?

(f) Is it true that a sardonic laugh is gay and cheerful?

(g) If you were too much excited to sleep, would a sedative probably help you?

(h) Is it true that a large elephant would be an encumbrance in an airplane?

(i) If a person makes a herculean effort, does he try hard or does he make almost no effort at all? Notice the preferred pronunciation of herculean.

(j) Why is it that no one has a predilection for cramps?

Section 60 has more questions for you to answer.

56
Idioms

An idiom is a group of words whose meaning cannot be guessed from mere knowledge of the meanings of the individual words. If the words are taken in their usual meanings, an idiom does not make sense.

Imagine yourself a foreigner, for instance, who is trying to learn English. You might know the meaning of *give* and *up*, but chances are that you would never be able to guess the meaning of the expression *to give up*, meaning "to stop trying." Here are four other idioms:

> *look out*— be careful:
>   look out for the dog
>
> *make up one's mind*— decide:
>   Make up your mind what you want
>
> *take off*— leave the ground:
>   The airplane took off at dawn.
>
> *put back*— return:
>   The boat put back into harbor.

Another interesting fact about idioms is that a single idiom often has several different meanings. *Take off*, for example, means "remove" (Take off your coat) or "imitate" (He takes off Charlie Chaplin very well) in addition to "leave the ground."

Here are some sentences containing idioms. Make a written list of them and briefly explain what they mean:

1. After the accident he lost his head completely.

2. The policeman made after the thief.

3. The Frenchman gave himself away by his accent.

4. He hung upon every word of the teacher.

5. The soldiers put down the rebellion.

6. He takes after his father.

7. She put by enough money to buy herself a new car.

Make written answers to these questions:

8. What idiom containing the word *take* means "to deceive"?

9. What does it mean to say that someone is a chip off the old block?

10. What idiom of two words, one of them being *come*, means "regain consciousness"?

You will find more about idioms in Section 66.

57

How Many Do You Know?

Match the words in the first column with their synonyms in the second column. Use each of the twelve words in the first column in a sentence of your own.

clarity	large hog
curvet	stubbornness; hardness of heart
fallow	course of study
marchioness	leap of a horse
curvature	bar of metal
mandate	command
obduracy	clearness
pigment	land left unseeded
queue	wife of a marquis
curriculum	division into hostile groups
ingot	long march
schism	pigtail
	saxophone
	spine
	coloring matter
	curving

Section 67 is the next which asks "How Many Do You Know?"

58

Latin

All the English words in each of the groups that follow are obviously related; all come from a single Latin word, and because of their realtionship to that word they make up a word-family.

In each group consider the connection between each of the words. See if you can find one idea that appears in all the words; if you can do so, you will then be able to tell the meaning of the Latin word from which the English word-family is derived.

After you have decided upon the meaning of the Latin parent of each word-family (The Latin word is given in parentheses at the end of each group), look up some of the words in a medium-size or large dictionary. You will then learn whether you have correctly guessed the meaning of the Latin word by referring to the etymological material given you there.

What does etymological mean?

(a) dictionary, dictate, dictograph, diction, contradict. Your problem is to guess the meaning of the Latin syllable *dict-,* a form of Latin *dicere*, which means "to........?"

(b) eject, project, projectile, projection, reject, object, interject, dejected. (What does *ject-* mean?)

(c) opponent, dispose, propose, repose, repository, expose, position, exposition, postpone. (*positum*, a form of *ponere*. What does *ponere* mean?)

(d) convalescent, valiant, valid, validate, invalid, valorous, prevalent, prevailing, valediction, avail, available (*valere*, to be................?)

Section 68 continues the study of Latin words.

59

Say and *Ask*

Say and *ask* turn up hundreds of times a day in speech and writing, yet there are other words that might be preferable. Here is a list of words meaning "say" that will be useful to you:

assert	maintain	suggest	blurt out
remark	insist	indicate	prattle
declare	contend	argue	shout
state	aver	testify	cry
protest	swear	utter	yell
allege	repeat	murmur	whisper
propose	observe	mutter	announce
hint	ejaculate	scream	reply

Write ten sentences using ten of these words properly and appropriately.

If you want to say "ask" and find yourself using *ask* over and over again, introduce a little variety into your writing and speech by using one of these expressions: *inquire, demand, want to know, question.* Some of the words meaning "say" in the list above, such as *argue, murmur, mutter, cry, blurt out*, *exclaim*, and *whisper*, can often be used effectively in the place of "ask".

Write five sentences in which you have substituted another word for *ask*.

60

Can You Answer These Questions?

(a) There is a dipthong in the word *noise*. Where is it?

(b) Is a snowfall in warm weather incongruous? Give an example of something else that is incongruous.

(c) Why is plagiarism usually considered dishonest?

(d) Why does the law penalize blackmail?

(e) Are forceps usually used by a postman, a football player, a surgeon, a soldier, or a streetcar conductor?

(f) Why is it usually unnecessary to prove the truth of an axiom?

(g) Is Christianity monotheistic or polytheistic?

(h) For a picnic would you prefer clement or inclement weather?

(i) "A flaccid balloon will come down soon." Why?

(j) Are soap and water efficacious against dirt? Why or why not?

Section 65 has more questions.

61

Prefixes

Here are some more common prefixes, together with their meaings:

equi-	equal
bi-	two
post-	after
trans-	across
poly-	many

What are the meanings of the following words? How does the prefix influence the meaning of the word? Use each word in a sentence.

(a) equidistant, equilateral, equilibrium, equipoise, equator, equivalent

(b) bicycle, biannual, billingual, bigamy, bimonthly

(c) post-war, posterity, postern, posthumous, postmortem, postscript

(d) transatlantic, transcontinental, transept, transfix, transit, translucent

(e) polysyllable, polytechnic, polygamy, polygon

Section 71 is the next which deals with prefixes.

62

Fifteen Words from
Kenilworth, by Sir Walter Scott

indulgence	intimated	injudicious
insolent	caustic	enhancing
alchemist	assiduous	habituated
votary	unbounded	demeanor
instigation	concurrence	factions

The fifteen words above have been extracted from the sentences below and have been replaced by synonymous words or hyphenated phrases. Put Scott's words back into their orginal places in the sentences by substituting each for its italicized synonym:

(a) After some brief interval, Master Goldthred, at the earnest *urging* of mine host, and the joyous *agreement* of his guests, indulged the company with the following morsel of melody.

(b) Elizabeth, like many of her sex, was fond of governing by *opposing-groups-of-persons*, so as to balance two opposing interests.

(c) The *student-of-chemical-magic made-known* his purpose to continue some experiment of high import during the greater part of the night.

(d) The unfortunate Countess of Leicester had, from her infancy upwards, been treated by those around her with *almost-too-much-kindness* as *unlimited* as it was *unwise*. The natural sweetness of her dispostion had saved her from becoming *boldly-rude* and ill-humored.

(e) During the banquets and revels which occupied the remainder of this eventful day, the bearing of Leicester and Varney was totally different from their usual *behavior*. Sir Richard Varney had been held rather a man of counsel and action, than a *devotee* of pleasure.

(f) If he exercised his wit, it was in a rough, *sarcastic*, and severe manner, rather as if he scoffed at the exhibition and the guests, than shared the common pleasure.

(g) It was entirely diffrent with Leicester. However *accustomed* his mind usually was to play the part of a good courtier, and appear gay, *diligent*, and free from all care but that of *increasing* the pleasure of the moment, his actions and gestures seemed like those of an automaton.

63

More Antonyms

In Section 53 we searched for antonyms, words that have meanings opposite to the meaning of another word. *Big* is the antonym of *little*, and *new* is the antonym of *old*.

Here are more antonyms. In the first column below are ten words. In the second column find one antonym for each of the ten words in the first column. With *destroy* in mind, for instance, run down the right-hand column until you find a word that means the opposite of *destroy*. Is it *repel*? *expand*? or *create*?

Do the same with the other words in the first column.

destroy	repel
contract	censure
attract	expand
follow	cut open
hasten	create
praise	join together
exult	suppose
concentrate	extol
anathemize	delay
cleave	diffuse
	precede

The Growing Vocabulary: Part Three

accompany
grieve deeply
loiter
travel
hurry
bless
look behind

Section 73 continues the discussion of antonyms.

64

True or False?

On a separate sheet of paper mark the following statements as true or false. Score your paper by the method suggested in Section 34.

1. Craftiness is skill in sailing a boat.

2. Epilepsy is a nervous disease.

3. *Irate* means "angry".

4. An obituary is a horse's harness.

5. Morphine is a drug which causes sleep.

6. An inferno is a place of torment.

7. Entomology is the study of insects.

8. *Omnivorious* means "eager to read everything."

9. Most people laugh at risible actions.

10. A testator is a test pilot for airplanes.

Section 74 also contains statements to be estimated as true or false.

65

More Questions

Can you answer these questions? You can if you know the meanings of the italicized words.

(a) Why is the study of *bacteriology* of more importance to surgeons than to aviators?

(b) Why is it that monkeys are unable to climb *genealogical* trees?

(c) Does it usually injure one physically to be *henpecked*? Why?

(d) What difference is there between an *impatient* person and an *impassive* person?

(e) Why should a politician not be *naive*?

(f) Poe wrote a story about a *purloined* letter. What do you think happened to the letter?

(g) What is wrong with *sniveling* when one has had a slight accident?

(h) Are sheep or eagles more *gregarious*?

(i) Is it true that California and Oregon are the *purlieus* of New York City? Explain why, or why not.

(j) What is the difference between a *prefix* and a *suffix*?

66

Idioms

Section 56 dealt with idioms, those expressive but often illogical phrases which, when considered word by word, fail to "make good sense." When taken together, however, idioms are easily understood by anyone who knows the English language well.

Here are fifteen sentences containing common idioms. Point out the idioms and tell the meaning of each sentence.

1. Political candidates usually steer clear of making definite promises.

2. This physician keeps abreast of the latest medical discoveries.

3. Travel in Asia is inexpensive if one knows the ropes.

4. The detective tried to ferret out the secret.

5. He is hard to do business with because he always beats about the bush.

6. His arrival was a bolt from the blue.

7. We liked to deal with him because he always laid his cards on the table.

8. My mother set her face against my leaving school.

9. He is badly injured, but the doctor says he will pull through.

10. Mary gets on well with all kinds of people.

11. He is not so strong as he was, for he is getting on in years.

12. He made bold to ask the actress for her autograph.

13. Keep him under your eye while you are in the museum.

14 He talked to us straight from the shoulder.

15. At the meeting he held forth at great length on his ambitions for the growth of the city.

Section 76 is the next which deals with idioms.

67

How Many Do You Know?

Match the words in the first column with their synonyms in the second column.

Use each of the words in the first column in a sentence of your own. Don't guess at the meaning of an unfamiliar word; look it up before you attempt to use it.

corpulence	watchword
comfit	small quantity
modicum	Arab chieftain
scarab	conversation
colloquy	army officer
shibboleth	short trip
elucidation	fatness
emir	luxury
imposture	gesture
inadequacy	explanation
jaunt	method
nonchalance	scar
	unconcern
	piece of candy
	beetle
	insufficiency
	plunge
	preacher
	deception, fraud

68

Latin

The words in each of the following groups or families are connected to each other in form and in meaning through the Latin word in parentheses.

Examine each group of words carefully, noticing how the meaning of the Latin word lingers in each English word but observing also how each English word differs in meaning from the others.

Proceed, process, procedure, procession, accede, accession, exceed, excessive, precedence (notice the pronunciation of this word), recede, recess (from Latin *cedere*, meaning "to go"; another form of this Latin word is *cessum*).

(a) What is the difference in meaning between *proceed* and *recede*?
Notice the difference in spelling.

(b) If a king has precedence over his lords when entering a banquet hall, who goes first?

Tractor, contract, attract, retract, trace, tractable (Latin *tractum*, from *trahere*, meaning "to drag").

(c) What is the difference between a tractable and an intractable horse?

(d) If a speaker retracts a statement, just what does he do?

Potent, potential, potentate, potency, potentiality, posse (From Latin *posse*, meaning "to be able," and *potens*, "powerful").

(e) Which is worse, a potent criminal or a potential criminal? How does the idea of power enter into both words?

(f) What is a potentate, and why is he so called?

Section 78 tells more about the influence of Latin on the English vocabulary.

69

Foreign Words and Phrases

Hundreds of words and phrases from Latin, French, German, Italian, Spanish, and Greek are frequently to be found in English writing and conversation. In this section and in Sections 79 and 89 are listed some of the phrases and words encountered most frequently.

à la carte	ordered from the bill-of-fare
anno Domini (A.D.)	in the year of our Lord
ante meridiem (A.M.)	before noon
au revoir	good-by
blitzkreig	lightning-like war
bon jour	good day, good morning
distrait	absent-minded
en route	on the way
ex libris	from the collection of books (of)
faux pas	social error
hoi polloi	the common people
in memoriam	in memory (of)
per annum	by the year
post meridiem (P.M.)	after noon
savoir faire	knowing how to do; social tact
table d' hôte	meal at a fixed price

via	by way of, through
via media	a middle way, avoiding extremes
vice versa	the other way around

(a) Learn by heart ten of the foreign words or phrases listed above.

(b) Use five of them in sentences of your own.

(c) Explain the meanings of these sentences:

Eating peas with a knife is a *faux pas*.

Meals *à la carte* are usually more expensive than *table d' hôte*.

People who have *savoir faire* seldom make *faux pas*.

He was *en route* to Denver *via* Chicago when the accident occurred.

If one finds a book marked "*Ex Libris* William Johnson" he should make an attempt to find the owner.

Section 79 contains more foreign words and phrases.

70

Some More Questions

It is indispensable to know the meanings of the italicized words if you are to answer the following questions. Don't guess at the meaning of a word; look it up!

(a) Are *nebulous* ideas an advantage when taking an examination? Why?

(b) Is it true that a rectangle is a *parallelogram*? Is a triangle a parallelogram?

(c) Why does a *mussel* need a strong muscle?

(d) Can you name five *predatory* animals or birds?

(e) Why would you be more surprised at the appearance of a *puma* in a college classroom than of a *pundit*?

(f) Why should a *debilitating* climate eventually cause the *decadence* of the people who live in it?

(g) Do you consider the statement that worms have no feathers to be *debatable*? Why?

(h) Why would the finding of a genuine *panacea* be disturbing to proprietors of drugstores?

Section 80 has more questions for you to answer.

71

Prefixes

The five prefixes that follow combine with other syllables to make words that are somewhat harder than those in Sections 51 and 61:

auto-	self
bene-	well
peri-	around
retro-	backwards, behind
tele-	afar

Use each of the following words in a sentence. Notice how the meaning of the prefix influences the meaning of the entire word:

(a) autobiography, autocrat, autograph, automaton, autonomous

(b) benediction, benevolent, beneficiary

(c) perimeter, periscope, periphery

(d) retrogress, retrospect

(e) telescope, television, telegraph, telephone, telepathy

72

Fifteen Words from
David Copperfield, by Charles Dickens

Translate these sentences into your own words, in such a way that you keep the original meaning without using any of the words that are italicized.

(a) Let us have no *meandering*.

(b) I was a *posthumous* child. My father's eyes had closed upon the light of this world six months, when mine opened upon it.

(c) There was an interval of silence, only broken by Miss Betsey's occasionally *ejaculating* "Ha!"

(d) I found there a stoutish, middle-aged person in a brown *surtout* and black tights and shoes.

(e) She would lay her hand upon her *nankeen* bosom.

(f) The old *anathemas* were made relishing on the same principle of several good words in succession for the expression of the same idea.

(g) It is not my intention to enter on a detailed list of the various *malpractices* of a minor nature, to which I have been a *tacitly* consenting party.

(h) I entered on a task of *clandestine* investigation.

(i) Mr. W. has been for years deluded and plundered to the *pecuniary* advantage of the *avaricious*, false, and grasping HEEP.

(j) These meshes were *perpetuated* by a miscellaneous catalogue of unscrupulous *chicaneries*.

(k) He proceeded to the *peroration* of his letter.

(l) It merely remains for me to *substantiate* these accusations.

73

Antonyms

Write answers to the following questions:

(a) If a man is the opposite of parsimonious, is he very small, generous, plutocratic, or disparaging?

(b) If you wished to attain the co-operation of your friends, would you avoid their companionship, good wishes, helpfulness, antagonism, or conversation?

(c) If you consider yourself loyal, which three of the following four words would you not use to describe yourself?—*traitorous, treasonable, faithful, false.*

(d) If you were having a debate with someone and he were to take the negative position, would you say that you were taking the posititve, the affirmative, the neglected, or the critical position?

(e) If someone were to deny that he is cowardly and were to insist that he is just the opposite, which three of the following words might he use to describe himself?—*valorous, timid, angry, intrepid, ambitious, violent, audacious, assiduous, virulent.*

The next section dealing with antonyms is Section 83.

74

True or False?

Using a separate sheet of paper, mark the following statements T or F, indicating that you think them true or false. Score the test as suggested in Section 34.

1. A guillotine is a coffee-grinder.

2. A deleterious substance is harmful.

3. Rigorous discipline is severe.

4. A dais is a raised platform.

5. A howitzer is a greeting meaning "hello."

6. Most canes have ferrules at the lower end.

7. Nocturnal events always occur in the daytime.

8. Eulogy is praise.

9. Postilions are rarer today than they were two hundred years ago.

10. A carnation is the crowning of a king or queen.

11. *Ironical* means made of iron.

12. Petulant children are more attractive than any others.

13. A slatternly woman usually looks untidy.

14. The pectoral muscles are in the forearm.

15. Hypercritical people seldom notice faults in others.

The next section containing sentences to be marked as true or false is Section 84.

75

Vocabulary Test on Part Three.
How Many Do You Know?

To take this test, follow the instructions in Section 25.

1. He gave us his *benediction*:
   money, signature, promise, coat, blessing

2. The *craftiness* of Ulysses:
   boat, cunning, weapons, friendliness, sayings

3. An *irate* old man:
   talkative, famous, gray-haired, angry, lovable

4. A long *obituary*:
   death-notice, bridle, orbit, tombstone, nail-file

5. He sat on the *dais*:
   hat, desk, platform, prow, beach

6. The king's *coronation*:
   robe, crowning, flower garden, speech, wife

7. *Curvature* of the spine:
   curving, rib, fracture, nerve, top end

8. Remarkable *obduracy*:
   endurance, stubbornness, kindliness,
   hopefulness, happiness

9. Changes in the *curriculum*:
   clock, river, course of study, crew, book

10. He kept his *equilibrium*:
    bicycle, money, hatred, balance, aquarium

11. *Antediluvian* creatures:
    queer-looking, grass-eating, ancient,
    small-headed, fat

12. He is *illiterate*:
    literary, ill, insignificant, repetitious,
    uneducated

13. Clever *machinations*:
    utensils, machines, gears, plots, jokes

14. Red *pigment*:
    coloring matter, hog, face, paper, sunset

15. The *purloined* letter:
    opened, soiled, famous, stolen, overweight

16. Beautiful *diction*:
    writing, enunciation, painting, sculpture,
    singing

17. A useful *panacea*:
    cure-all, kettle, piece of information, book, tool

18. *Intrepid* soldiers:
    cowardly, fast-moving, laughing, ruthless,
    bold

19. A large *howitzer*:
    hotel, firecracker, milk-can, bomb, cannon

20. A great *monarch*:

monolith, march, fight, king, truth

21. A small *gimlet*:
    nail, boy, clearance, gift, boring tool

22. *Sagacious* advice:
    wise, bad, hurtful, thoughtless, expensive

23. A *valorous* soldier:
    tired, wounded, well-armed, brave,
    fast-marching

24. A feeble *mendicant*:
    excuse, beggar, muscle, old woman, little child

25. A *bigoted* opponent:
    important, sarcastic, prejudiced,
    unsportsmanlike, exhausted.

A key to this test will be found on page 179.

The
Growing
Vocabulary
Fun and Adventure with Words

Part Four

76

Idioms

A famous English writer, Walter Savage Landor, once declared that "every good writer has much idiom; it is the life and spirit of language." If you are eager to learn to write lively and spirited language, you should make a point of using idiom. Otherwise your writing and speaking are liable to be rather dull and lifeless.

The Sherlock Holmes stories are lively pieces of writing, and you will find that the author, Sir Arthur Conan Doyle, uses idiom continually. If you do not know the Sherlock Holmes stories, get hold of the volumes entitled *The Adventures of Sherlock Holmes*, *The Memoirs of Sherlock Holmes*, and *The Return of Sherlock Holmes*. You will also enjoy *The Hound of the Baskervilles*, a long story in which the great detective plays the leading part.

Here are some idioms of the kind that abound in Sir Arthur Conan Doyle's characteristic writing. Be sure you know what they mean, and then use each of the idioms in sentences of your own composition. Make a practice of using some of these same idioms in your own writing and speaking.

The Growing Vocabulary: Part Four

1. The cooking is hopeless: you will have *to give the cook notice.*

2. Success has *turned many a man's head.*

3. If a *cry of fire is raised*, the crowd will always *take it up.*

4. I was completely *taken in* by his disguise.

5. It's a poor sport who *makes merry* over an accident to an opponent.

6. One thinks twice before *falling foul of* an armed desperado.

7. The significance of the news *came home to* him suddenly and *struck cold to his heart.*

8. As soon as he opened the gate, the dog *flew upon* him.

9. Of late, when he was *in his cups*, the mention of her name would make him *beside himself* with fury.

10. Keep a sharp look-out! Before an hour's gone by, we'll *lay him by the heels.*

Section 86 contains more idioms.

77

British and American

Many English words and expressions are "local"—used in one district but not in another. The differences may have been caused in the past by natural barriers which prevented free movement in the days when travel was far harder than it is now. Local words are common in England—and in English literature—where communities have often been settled for centuries without much movement of their people; in America—and in American literature— local words are perhaps rarer, but they are not hard to find.

The Atlantic both joins and separates the American and the British people. Anyone moving in either direction across the Atlantic will soon notice the differences in words used to express the same idea (for instance a "mail-box" in the United States is a "pillar-box" in England); he will also notice different shades of meaning for the same word. Since we in this country share a common language with the English and since we naturally read much English literature, it is well to be aware of some of the differences in our vocabularies.

Let us look at further examples. *Locomotives* are

driven by *engineers* in the United States, but a British "engineer" would think it beneath him to drive an "engine." He leaves that work to a British "engine-driver," assisted by a "stoker," while an English "fireman" puts out fires and has no connection whatever with "railways."

Such differences as these are rapidly disappearing under the influence of the movies and the radio, and American expressions (until a few years ago most commonly found in Stratford-on-Avon, because of the extraordinarily large number of American visitors to Shakespeare's birthplace) are now well known throughout the British Isles. Hence there may be many differences of opinon as to whether a particular word may be labeled Britsh or American.

In England	In the United States
petrol	gasoline
windscreen	windshield
bonnet (of a car)	hood
paraffin	kerosene
torch	flashlight
lorry	truck
truck (for luggage)	handcart
guard (of a train)	conductor
goods train	*freight train
lift	* elevator

* Freight train and elevator are terms that have come into common use in England only in the last few years.

Section 87 tells of other differences in British and American vocabularies.

78
Latin

Sometimes one needs to know the meaning of *two* Latin words to understand thoroughly the meaning of an English word. From list B (below), bulid up the literal meanings of the English words in List A. Compare your results with the definitions given in a good dictionary; you will then have a clear idea of how helpful a knowledge of Latin is in the buliding of English vocabulary.

A

benediction, benefactor, benevolent
malefactor, malevolent
equilateral, equinox, equanimity, equilibrium
bisect, trisect, biennial
agriculture
anniversary

B

aequus (equ-)	equal, even
ager (agr-)	field
animus (anim-)	mind
annus (anni-)	year

bene	well
bi-	two
cultus, from *colere*	to cultivate
dictum, from *dicere*	to speak
factum, from *facere*	to do, to make
male	badly, ill
nox	night
later-, from *latus*	side
sectum, from *secare*	to cut
tri-	three, triple
libra	balance
versus, from *vertere*	to turn
volens	willing, wishing

(a) What is a benediction at the end of a church service?

(b) Would most people prefer to be benefactors or malefactors?

(c) Would you rather have a benevolent father or a malevolent one?

(d) What is an equilateral triangle?

(e) Is equanimity a desirable quality? Why?

(f) What is the difference in meaning between *biannual* and *biennial*?

79

More Foreign Words and Phrases

ad libitum (ad lib.)	as one pleases
bête noire	object of hatred
camouflage	disguise
carte blanche	unrestricted permission
casus belli	sufficient cause for war
débutante	girl making first appearance
entente cordiale	friendly understanding
fiancé(e)	one's betrothed
joie de vivre	pleasure in living
menu	list of food served
nom de plume	pseudonym, "pen-name"
per diem	daily, by the day
post mortem	after death; examination after death
prima donna	leading woman singer in an opera
pro tempore (pro tem.)	for the time being
re	with regard to
rendezvous	meeting place
status quo	existing state of affairs
verbatim	word for word

(a) What does an actor do when he "*ad libs*" in a play?

(b) Do you know two countries between which there is an *entente cordiale*?

(c) Do you know Samuel L. Clemens' *nom de plume*?

(d) Conservatives usually wish to preserve the *status quo*. What does this mean?

(e) Shorthand writers should make an effort to record *verbatim* everything said in court. If this statement is true, how many words may such a shorthand writer omit?

(f) *Camouflage* is a French word that made its appearance in English during World War I. Do you know any other words or phrases, either French or German, that have appeared in our language as a result of the World War, of the Second World War, or of recent political conditions?

Section 89 gives a further list of foreign words and phrases.

80

Can You Answer These Questions?

(a) Which would you rather find in your garden, an azalea or an anaconda? Why?

(b) What is the difference between the snarling of a dog and the snarling of a fish-line?

(c) Why is it unlikely that a small boy would hector the captain of a school football team?

(d) What kind of people would you expect to read about in Thackeray's *Book of Snobs*?

(e) Why is blarney often an asset to a politician?

(f) If you were hungry, why should you prefer to receive succotash rather than balderdash?

(g) Is a gendarme a policeman, a fireman, a lawyer, a general, or a college professor?

(h) Why are gargoyles uncommunicative?

(i) "G.K. Chesteron was a master of paradox." What does that statement mean?

(j) "A stitch in time saves nine." Is that statement an epidemic, an epidermis, an epiglottis, an epigram, or an epilogue?

More questions are asked in Section 90.

81

Families of Words

Here are some families of words all of whose members you ought to know. If you do not know the meaning of one of the words, look it up. Then use it in your conversation or writing just as soon as you can find an opportunity to do so.

Write sentences, using at least one word from each family. Choose the least familiar words rather than ones which you already know well.

(a) evade, evasive, evasion, evader

(b) literature, literal, literate, illiteracy

(c) contact, contagious, contingency, contiguous

(d) decay, deciduous, decadence

(e) manifest, manifesto, manifestation

(f) ostensible, ostensibly, ostentation, ostentatious

(g) moment, momentous, momentum, momentary

(h) virus, virulent

(i) mandate, mandatory

(j) propitiate, propitiation, propitious

(k) protract, protraction, protractor, protracted

(l) diversify, divers, diverse, diversity, diversification

Section 91 is the next which deals with Families of Words.

82
Greek

We live in a time when science dominates our physical and our mental lives. Thousands of the common and the uncommon terms of science—of biology, physics, chemistry, astronomy, geology, zoology, botany, medicine, and so on—derive directly from Greek. In other words, the study of Greek has never before been so useful in a practical way as it now is; yet never before has the study of Greek been so neglected in American schools and colleges.

In this section, and in Section 92, are a few common Greek words and roots, a knowledge of which will help you to understand and remember Greek derived words, especially scientific ones.

bios, life: amphibious, biography, biology, biogenesis

kratos, might: autocrat, democrat, plutocrat

gamos, marriage: monogamy, bigamy, polygamy

genos, race: genealogy, genesis

grapho, write: telegraph, photograph, auto-
          graph, biography, geography

helios, sun: helium, heliograph,
          heliocscope, heliotrope

logos, reason, word, understanding: logic,
          philology, geology, zoology

meter, measure: thermometer, barometer,
          metric system, centimeter,
          mircrometer

(a) Frogs live both on land and in the water. Are they properly termed *amphibious*?

(b) Do the laws of the United States favor monogamy, bigamy, or polygamy?

(c) What is a helioscope?

(d) If *micro-* means "small," what is a micrometer?

(e) From each group of words above select the one that is least familiar, look it up, and then write it in a sentence.

Section 92 continues the study of Greek words and roots which appear with some frequency in English words.

83

Antonyms

(a) If the President vetoes a proposal of Congress, does he refuse to retract it, remove it, perceive it, enlist it, or endorse it?

(b) One of the following words is the opposite of *adversary*. Which is it? *Collaborator, opponent, criminal, insect, spellbinder.*

(c) Is a spurious document the opposite of one which is genuine, ancient, outrageous, illegal, or impracticable?

(d) *Infamous* is not a true antonym of *famous*. What does *infamous* mean? What is an accurate antonym of *famous*?

(e) *In-* prefixed to a word often suggests the opposite idea: it means "not." *Inaccurate*, for instance, means "not accurate," *informal* means "not formal," and *involuntary* means "not voluntary."

Not all words, however, which begin with *in-* contain the idea of "not"; not all such words have as their antonyms the same words shorn of *in-*. *Inane*, for instance, means "silly" or "empty"; but there is no such word as *ane*.

Which of the following words form antonyms by dropping the prefix *in-*? *Inaccessible, inadvertent, inarticulate, incapacitate, incense, incompatible, incredulous,* and *indigent.* What does each of these words mean?

(f) Open a medium-size dictionary to the pages containing words begining with *in-*; select some of these words at random and determine whether the same word with *in-* omited is in good usage as an antonym.

(g) What is the difference in meaning between

habitable and *inhabitable* (Don't guess; you will make an error if you do!)

inhabitant and *habitant*

heritable and *inheritable*

insnare and *snare* (verb)

tegument and *integument*

trust and *intrust*

valuable and *invaluable*

84

True or False?

Mark the following statements T or F to indicate that you think them true of false. Whenever you mark a statement false, give your reason for so doing.

1. Finesse is skill or craftiness.

2. A lugubrious voice is sad and mournful.

3. A flamingo is a forest fire.

4. A reprimand is a rebuke.

5. A termagant is a quarreling, scolding woman.

6. An impecunious person has little or no money.

7. Stringent laws are strict laws.

8. Few people care to be ostracized.

9. *Dyspepsia* means "good digestion."

10. Astuteness is sagacity.

11. To abrogate a law is to do away with it.

12. *Abscond* means "steal." (Be sure to look up *abscond*.)

13. Destitution is great wealth.

14. Gentians are charming people who live in the hills of Pennsylvania.

15. Impolitic actions are usually injudicious.

16. *Transparent, translucent,* and *opaque* are synonymous.

17. Copper wire is ductile.

18. The solar plexus is a bone in the elbow.

19. A privateer was a kind of warship owned by private persons.

20. *Sahib,* a word used frequently in Kipling's Indian stories, means "sir" or "master".

Section 94 has more sentences to be marked true or false.

85

Adjectives and Nouns

Write the nouns which correspond to the following adjectives. Use each noun in a sentence of your own compostion.

episodic	irascible
sacrilegious	morbid
irresolute	prescient
treasonous	rustic
monosyllabic	literate
intuitive	ebullient
gymnastic	stealthy

Section 95 deals with pairs of verbs and nouns.

86
Idioms

Column I contains fifteen common idioms; column II contains, in different order and mingled with irrelevant material, the meanings of the fifteen idioms.

Match the idioms with their meanings by setting side by side the proper numeral and the proper letter.

If, for instance, you think that *to bear a hand* means "to remove one's glove," write "2 n."

Use each idiom in a sentence that will show the meaning of the idiom.

I	**II**
1. to take alarm	a. to retreat
2. to bear a hand	b. to listen
3. to come a cropper	c. to lower the pride of
4. to eat one's heart out	d. to tell the time
5. to breed ill blood	e. to raise vegetables
6. to make a clean breast	f. to become frightened
7. to lend an ear	g. famous
8. to be in hot water	h. to stir up bad feeling
9. to be off	i. to fail
10. to bear back	j. to give aid quickly
11. to take someone down	k. to wash one's neck and chest

12. to take to one's heels
13. to fall through
14. on one's uppers
15. down in the mouth

l. to fall, to have a setback
m. poverty-stricken
n. to remove one's glove
o. to remove from a shelf
p. to be in trouble
q. to grieve deeply
r. to carry something in a knapsack
s. to depart
t. to offer
u. to confess everything
v. to run away
w. depressed, unhappy

The next section concerning Idioms is Section 96.

87

British and American

English children like *sweets* and clean their faces with *wash-rags*. In wet weather they usually wear *mackintoshes* and *boots*; *shoes* and *galoshes* are less popular. Their beds are covered with *counterpanes*. They have *porridge* for breakfast, *biscuits* in the middle of the morning, and *pudding* for the second course at lunch, though *tinned* fruit is popular. If they are thirsty, they may drink from the *tap*. In the cities British children are more likely to go to school by *tram* than by *motor-car*; in London, many travel by *Underground*, but they never walk along the *railway-lines* or step on the *sleepers*. At *playtime* one often sees them playing with *knuckle-bones* or *skipping rope*. They enjoy the *cinema* just as much as their American cousins.

The passage above contains many expressions (all of them italicized) which are peculiar to the speech of the British Isles or are more frequently found in use there than in the United States. Below are the twenty-one expressions used most commonly in America instead of the expressions used in the passage.

The American expressions listed below are not in the same order in which they occur in the paragraph above. You will have little trouble, however, in puzzling out just what is meant in each case.

Make a list in two columns of the British expresssions and the equivalent American expressions.

recess	low shoes	jacks
dessert	streetcar	raincoats
the subway	cereal	canned
candy	movies	bedspreads
automobile	high shoes	crackers
tracks	face-cloths	ties
rubbers	faucet	jumping rope

Section 97 concludes the discussion of British and American expressions.

88

Dozens of Words

Perhaps by the time you have reached this point in *The Growing Vocabulary*, you have the impression that the writers must be running out of words. There is no such likelihood; an unabridged dictionary holds half a million words. Many of these words, of course, are archaic, obsolescent, obsolute, techincal, poetic, vulgar, dialect, slangy, or otherwise not of immediate interest. Hundreds of words remain, however, which you probably do not know and which will be useful to you in expressing your ideas and in enlarging your experience. Here are three dozen of them; they are purposely made difficult.

In the first column you will find thirty-six definitions; in the second column you will find a word to correspond to the definition (this words is never farther off then five words above or below the definition).

Match the definitions in the first column with the corresponding word in the second column.

Opposite the middle of a ship	abstruse
Occuring here and there	savanna
Hard to understand	lese majesty

A treeless plain	abeam
The equipment of a soldier	adjuration
Treason against the sovereign	aesthetic
A solemn command or appeal	sporadic
A center of attention or interest	amalgam
The study of insects	stratification
Never changing	accouterments
Artistic, or connected with beauty	immutable
To put into prison	entomology
An alloy one part of which is mercury	cynosure
Arrangement in layers	anthropology
To make unfavorable criticisms	fusillade
Study of the development of mankind	purulent
The firing of many firearms at one time	incarcerate
A two-wheeled carriage drawn by a man	scantling
Full of pus	apostasy
A small piece of timber	animadvert
Abandonment of one's religion	importune
Unreasonably zealous or enthusiastic	jinricksha
To demand urgently or repeatedly	archaeology
A severe headache	spheroid
The study of anicent cities, etc.	premeditated
The wild or half-wild American horse	fanatical
A protection against disease	migraine
Resembling a ball in shape	prophylactic
Planned beforehand	autocracy
Rule by an unrestricted monarch	mustang
A granite-like rock	bombast
A sea-nymph	gneiss

High-sounding but
    empty language   imbroglio
Doubtful of the truth about
    apparent facts   nereid
Roman tax-collector   skeptical
A complex misunderstanding   publican

89

Foreign Words and Phrases

auf Widersehen	good-bye
billet-doux	short love-letter
carpe diem	enjoy the present moment
cause célèbre	celebrated law case
cul de sac	blind alley
élite	the choicest part of society
entre nous	between ourselves
ersatz	artificial substitute
ex cathedra	offically
ex officio	by virtue of the position or office
gauche	clumsy, that one holds tactless
gendarme	policemen
hors de combat	disabled; out of the fight
in camera	in secret
in medias res	into the midst of things
lebensraum	space in which to live
mal-de-mer	seasickness
obiter dicta	casual remarks
pièece de résistance	chief dish of a dinner
prima facie	at first glance
raison d'être	excuse for existing
rara avis	rare bird; unusual kind of person, etc.

sang froid	calmness, imperturbability of mind
sine die	indefinitely
tête-à-tête	face to face; private conversation
tour de force	feat of skill
trek	journey, migration; to travel

(a) Certain Greek and Roman philosophers preached a doctrine of *carpe diem*. What did they urge people to do?

(b) *Gauche* is the French word for "left-handed"; how does it come to mean "clumsy" or "tactless"?

(c) When a story is said to plunge "*in medias res*," what does that mean?

(d) What is *prima facie* evidence of murder?

(e) Do you agree that a blue giraffe is a *rara avis*?

(f) Why is *sang froid* valuable in an emergency?

(g) When the Senate adjourns *sine die*, when does it plan to meet again?

This is the last section dealing solely with Foreign Words and Phrases. Section 98, however, contains a few more such words and phrases which are in common use.

Keep on the lookout for foreign words and phrases in your reading. If they are unfamiliar to you, look them up in a dictionary. At the back of most dictionaries there is a special glossary of foreign words and phrases.

90

More Questions

(a) What happens when a hue and cry is raised?

(b) Explain briefly one occasion on which you have cogitated.

(c) Why does one have to be literate to read a book?

(d) Why is procrastination called "the thief of time"?

(e) Why is it rare to find many longshoremen on a ship in the middle of the ocean?

(f) Why would you probably object to having a layman operate upon you for appendicitis?

(g) Why would most people find it trying to live in a pandemonium?

(h) Why is it that one can inherit nothing from posterity?

(i) Why is the usual motion of a snake called sinuous?

(j) Why would it not damage your watch to synchronize it with another watch?

(k) Why is it usually considered preferable to graduate from college *magna cum laude* rather than *cum laude*?

(l) Do you have any *amour-propre*? If not, don't you think you should have?

(m) Why is a square not a rhombus?

(n) What word begining *spo-* and containing three more letters means either "husband" or "wife"?

(o) Why does decapitation always kill a person?

91
Families of Words

In each of the following groups of related words, find at least one which is either new or only vaguely familiar to you. After looking up its meaning, write it in an appropriate sentence:

(a) inflame, inflammation, inflammatory, inflamed

(b) character, characteristic, characterize

(c) dispute, disputation, disputatious, disputable, indisputable

(d) jubilant, jubilation, jubilce

(e) moral, morality, moralist, moralize, morale

(f) deprave, depraved, depravity

(g) pestilence, pestiferous, pestilent, pestilential

(h) jury, jurisdiction, jurisprudence, juryman, jurist

(i) heterodox, heterogeneous

(j) equalization, equalizer, equanimity, equate, equatorial

92
Greek

Here are a few more Greek words and roots (see Section 82) which are useful in understanding and remembering certain English words, especially scientific ones.

Look up the meaning of any word that you do not know. Use every word in a sentence that will show its meaning.

optikos, visual:
optic, optician, optometry

pathos, suffering:
pathetic, pathology, antipathy, sympathy, pathos

petros, rock:
petrography, petrify, petroleum, petrology

hydor, water:
hydroaeroplane, hydrant, hydroelectric,
hydraulic, hydrogen, hydrodynamics,
hydrometer, hydrophobia

chronos, time:
chronology, chronometer, anachronism,
chronicle, synchronize, isochronous

demos, the common people:
democracy, demagogue

93

Idioms

One of the chief sources of idioms in English is the human body. One can keep his *head* in an emergency, split *hairs* in an argument, fly in the *face* of facts, twist someone round his *finger*, be on his last *legs*, take someone in *hand*, take to his *heels*, set a scheme on *foot*, know a poem by *heart*, *back* out of a promise, and be up to one's *neck* in trouble.

    (a) Here are some idioms which include the word *head*. What does each mean? Use each in sentence:
to lose one's head
to come to a head
to talk one's head off
to put it into someone's head
to be out of one's head
to have one's head turned

    (b) What other idioms can you think of that contain the word *head*? You should be able to think of two or three more.

    (c) A good many idioms contain the word *face*. Here are a few. Write each in a sentence.

to have the face to
to set one's face against
to face someone down
to face something out
to put a good face upon

(d) The word *eye* enters into many idioms:
to be all eyes
to have an eye to
to have an eye for
to turn a blind eye to
an eye for an eye
more than meets the eye

94

True or False?

See Section 34 for instructions on scoring this test. When you consider a statement false, explain why.

1. *Ingenuous* means "naive."

2. Verdant hills are brown and dry.

3. A hilarious party is usually noisy.

4. Tantrums are charming.

5. Decorum is a form of decoration for churches.

6. It is disgraceful to be a public benefactor.

7. Great public speakers are not likely to be incoherent.

8. *Incipient* means "in an early stage," "just beginning."

9. Earthworms are flamboyant creatures.

10. One copeck equals two quarts.

11. *Meticulous* means "very careful."

12. A parasite is the same as a hypocrite.

13. Comely people are always uncouth.

14. *To dissuade* is the opposite of *to persurade*.

15. To precipitate a war is to prevent it.

16. A vanguard is an armed policeman who protects a motor truck.

17. Taciturn people usually speak very little.

18. A peregrination is a journey.

19. A stalagmite and a stalactite are precisely the same thing.

20. A folio is larger that an octavo.

95
Verbs and Nouns

What noun corresponds to each of the following verbs? Write your answers in two columns, one for the verbs and the other for the corresponding nouns. Use each of the nouns in a sentence.

jeopardize	rhapsodize
ostracize	gibber
preponderate	liquefy
eulogize	protrude
disparage	purvey
lacerate	reciprocate

96
Idioms

One can form many hundreds of English idioms from such common verbs as

come	fall	take	put
go	stand	look	set
run	get	lay	do
keep	hold	pull	make

by combining them with such common prepositions and adverbs as

above	away	for	over
about	back	from	through
across	before	in	to
after	behind	of	under
against	below	off	up
along	by	on	upon
at	down	out	with

Take, for example, combines with certain of these prepositions to make these idioms:

take after	—pursue; look like or act like
take down	—lower pride; remove, write, swallow
take in	—earn; deceive; receive; absorb; understand; shorten
take off	—mimic; remove
take on	—undertake, show grief or agitation
take over	—acquire (a responsibility, etc.) from another
take up	—absorb; tighten; lift; begin
take to	—like
take away	—remove
take back	—recover; receive again; retract (a statement)
take out	—remove

You will notice that many idioms have more than one meaning. *Get on*, as a further example, has various meanings illustrated in these sentences:

He got on the horse. (mounted)
He got on well with Bob. (was on good terms)
He got on well in business. (prospered)
As one gets on, his hair becomes white. (grows old)

Take each of the verbs, one by one, that are listed at the beginning of this section and combine them with the listed adverbs and prepositions. Write down all the idioms that you recognize, and after each idiom write its meaning. Keep a close watch for idioms that have two or more meanings. You should find at least fifty idioms.

97

British and American

As in Section 87, replace the italicized word (commonly used in England and in English writing) with a word that is more familiar to the average American and which is contained in this list:

soft cotton cloth	sick
notions	adults
drugstore	clerks
fabric store	spool of thread
raw cotton	grain
tavern	printed cloth
ocean	vests
vegetable man	yardage
dish-towels	basting
corn	hope chest

Grown-ups, like children, are much the same on both sides of the *sea*, though they may use different words for the same thing. When baby is *ill*, the English mother goes to the *chemist's shop*.

If she needs material for making her own *tea- cloths*, she will get it at the *draper's* where the *shop-assistants* are supposed to know the difference between *flannelette* and *calico*; they would not sell a customer *cotton-wool* for *tacking*, when she obviously wants a *reel-of-cotton*. The *smallwear* counter is always convenient; a girl has to think of everything when she has a *bottom-drawer* to fill.

Any *greengrocer* will tell you that he does not sell *corn* and that the climate in England is not warm enough to ripen *maize*. Farmhands usually take off their coats but keep on their *waistcoats* while at work; in the evenings they talk politics in local *public house*.

Note: *Certain words above (like reel-of-cotton and bottom-drawer) are hyphenated to show that for the purposes of this section they are to be considered as one word. In actual usage shop assistants, cotton wool, reel of cotton, chemist's shop, bottom drawer, and public house would be printed without hyphens.*

98

More Dozens of Words

Below you will find nine sets of a dozen words (or phrases). Each group of twelve words consists of six pairs of synonyms.

Collect the pairs of synonyms and write them together. When you finish, you should have fifty-four pairs of words.

I	II	III
insane	chic	wraith
prediction	ennui	wheedle
educated	stylish	evaporating rapidly
demented	legerdemain	revile
erudite	sub rosa	specter
untrue	vis-à-vis	of great size
black	prestidigitation	coax
sable	face to face	voluminous
prognostication	weariness	vituperate
salacious	scullion	glassy
fallacious	kitchen servant	vitreous
obscene	confidentially	volatile

IV	V	VI
ulster	viscous	swollen
trice	trepidation	ghoul
throe	ewer	unwise
agony	sticky	matriculate
purveyance	gratuitous	speak evil of
overcoat	violent storm	enroll as a
		student
major-domo	water-pitcher	moiety
very short time	fear	vilify
provisions	typhoon	turgid
steward	irksome	part
germinate	tedious	injudicious
sprout	tree	grave robber

VII	VIII	IX
vertex	reduplicate	mediocre
petulant	repeat	vassalage
refulgent	secrete	of ordinary
		quality
inequitable	verbosity	prowess
peevish	sirocco	pusillanimous
highest point	hide	profligate
splendid	hot, dry wind	servitude
scurrilous	wordiness	bravery
sear	sterility	very wicked
abusive	feeler	risible
withered	barrenness	laughable
unfair	tentacle	cowardly

99

A Word Bee

If you are using this book in a classroom, you can have a Word Bee. A Word Bee is conducted like a Spelling Bee. Your teacher will formulate the rules and announce them to you.

Below are a hundred words, all previously given to you in this book, which will be useful in a Word Bee.

(To the teacher: Previous notice may be given that a Word Bee is to be held and opportunity may be offered to study the hundred words listed below; or the Word Bee may be held without preliminary announcement.

Contestants should be asked not only the meaning of a word but should be required to use it in an appropriate sentence or otherwise show a knowledge of the usage of the word.)

perpetuity	audibly	quadrille	rivulet
portmanteau	apprehensive	divulge	diverge
culprit	rabies	diligence	missile
paragon	pentagon	infidel	cornea
surplice	binnacle	annuity	malignant
indemnity	vesture	squalid	avaricious

preachment	zenith	obsequious	duenna
obese	imbecility	crass	exemplary
spurious	rebus	mausoleum	conjecture
machination	usurer	dexterous	felicity
buccaneer	contiguous	vociferous	subterraneous
antediluvian	antitoxin	monomania	sagacious
oblique	reprobate	felicitate	morion
herculean	mandate	ingot	etymological
valediction	forceps	efficacious	bilingual
transept	polysyllable	instigation	concurrence
enhance	anathematize	irate	entomology
omnivorous	testator	genealogy	impassive
gregarious	purlieu	corpulence	colloquy
elucidate	nonchalance	tractable	potential
savoir faire	nebulous	predatory	pundit
panacea	automaton	periphery	assiduous
deleterious	ferrule	postilion	ironical
slattern	pectoral	equanimity	biennial
gargoyle	paradox	epigram	micrometer

100

Vocabulary Test on Part Four.
How Many Do You Know?

For instructions on how to take this test, see Section 25.

1. *Reprimand* the boy:
   reward, whip, rebuke, laugh at, help

2. *Contiguous* countries:
   neighboring, defeated, ancient, diseased, flat

3. Much *ostentation*:
   modesty, showiness, education, light,
   truthfulness

4. A *snarled* fishing-line:
   silk, tarred, tangled, short, thick

5. He talks *balderdash*:
   French, slang, business, nonsense, fast

6. A *demented* woman:
   happy, young, aged, weak, crazed

7. A shrewd *prognostication*:
   politician, doctor, prediction, lawyer, thief

8. *Erudite* scholars:
   pedantic, gray-haired, famous, foreign,
   learned

9. In *jeopardy*:
   danger, jail, trouble, war, foreign, lands

10. A *lacerated* face:
    beautiful, cut, fat, sallow, ambitious

11. *Meticulous* handwriting:
    slanting, illegible, minute, large, careful

12. A *disputatious* fellow:
    angry, argumentative, unhealthy, friendly, brave

13. Extreme *depravity*:
    heat, wickedness, stupidity, old age, fury

14. Ask the *gendarme*:
    fireman, clerk, priest, laundryman,
    policeman

15. A great *philologist*:
    refrigerator, student of language, biologist,
    Biblical student, lover

16. *Stringent* regulations:
    strict, brief, ancient, easy, stupid

17. The King's *manifesto*:
    robes, adviser, proclamation, death, wife

18. *Flamboyant* decorations:
    badly designed, pretty, old, soiled, gaudy

19. *Benevolent* people:
    sick, wealthy, poor, kindly, shrewd

20. Remarkable *equanimity*:
    ferocity, honesty, graciousness, calm,
    activity

21. He graduated *cum laude*:
    with praise, in three years, in five years,
    with low marks, unexpectedly

22. To *eulogize* the dead:
    mourn for, remember, bury, think of, praise

23. A *petulant* child:
    well-dressed, thin, peevish, gay, truthful

24. *Scurrilous* remarks:
    abusive, truthful, stupid, brilliant, many

25. A *risible* action:
    outrageous, deliberate, rapid, laughable,
    terrible

A key to this test will be found on page 179.

The
Growing
Vocabulary

Fun and Adventure with Words

Keys to the
Vocabulary Tests

Section 25

1. convincing
2. eternal
3. occupation
4. yearly payment
5. ended
6. trunk
7. stubborn
8. traveling-bag
9. hateful
10. polite
11. sad
12. villain
13. ghost
14. detestable
15. watchful
16. bill
17. lawyer
18. fearful
19. clamorous
20. question
21. fundamentals
22. united
23. similar
24. malicious
25. industriously

Section 50

1. dismay
2. fat
3. hates
4. rest
5. happiness
6. skillful
7. flexible
8. deserving
9. steep
10. theft
11. hopeful
12. talkative
13. greedy
14. small hill
15. apron
16. center
17. angered
18. clothing
19. underground
20. foreign
21. dishonest
22. rainfall
23. pale
24. stealthy
25. invincible

Section 75

1. blessing
2. cunning
3. angry
4. death-notice
5. platform
6. crowning
7. curving
8. stubbornness
9. course of study
10. balance
11. ancient
12. uneducated
13. plots
14. coloring-matter
15. stolen

16. enunciation
17. cure-all
18. bold
19. cannon
20. king
21. boring tool
22. wise
23. brave
24. beggar
25. prejudiced

Section 100

1. rebuke
2. neighboring
3. showiness
4. tangled
5. nonsense
6. crazed
7. prediction
8. learned
9. danger
10. cut
11. careful
12. argumentative
13. wickedness
14. policeman
15. student of language

16. strict
17. proclamation
18. gaudy
19. kindly
20. calm
21. with praise
22. praise
23. peevish
24. abusive
25. laughable

The
Growing
Vocabulary

Fun and Adventure with Words

Keys to the
Exercises

The Growing Vocabulary

The following "answers" to the exercises are meant to be suggestive, not exhaustive. The omission of keys to certain sections or parts of sections is deliberate; to supply such keys would defeat the purpose of the exercise. Use a dictionary.

Exercise 1

(a) induce someone to do or to believe
    act or power of persuading
(b) join together
    condition of being united
    to make into one
    act of uniting, union
(c) eternal, continuous
    to make perpetual
    eternal existence
(d) to ruin, spoil, end, kill
    ruin
    tending to destroy, causing destruction, ruinous
    destructive person or thing (also kind of
        warship)
        able to be destroyed
(e) to plot secretly with others to do
        something wrong
    secret plotting with others to do wrong
    plotter

The Growing Vocabulary

Exercise 2

Since Alice was concerned with *latitude* and *longitude* merely as words, it is impossible to substitute their meanings without injuring the sense of the sentence. Although Alice had not the slightest idea of their meaning, we should know that

latitude is distance measured north or south of the equator on the earth's surface, and that
longitude is distance measured east or west of Greenwich on the carth's surface.
ventured—dared, took the risk (of tasting)
adjourn—stop for a time
adoption　selection, choosing
remedies—cures
audibly—loud enough to be heard
suppressed—put down by force, stopped by force
consultation—conference, meeting to talk or
　　　　　　　　discuss
familiarly—in a friendly, intimate way
quadrille—a square dance

Exercise 3

happy—gay, delighted, content, cheerful, glad,
　　　　blissful, overjoyed, enraptured, blithe,
　　　　joyful, joyous, etc.
brave—bold, audacious, intrepid, courageous,
　　　　daring, etc.
tired—weary, exhausted, worn-out, etc.

pretty—beautiful, lovely, exquisite, fetching, comely, etc.
old—ancient, aged, antique, antiquated, superannuated,
    hoary, venerable, aboriginal, antediluvian, etc.
unhappy—sad, miserable, depressed, dejected,
          cheerless, joyless, melancholy, glum, etc.
strong—powerful, potent, vigorous, muscular, sturdy,
    etc.
afraid—frightened, terrified, timid, fearful, etc.
little—tiny, minute, microscopic, small, diminutive,
    puny, dwarfish, pygmy, atomic, infinitesimal,
    molecular, etc.
intelligent—brilliant, smart, bright, acute, keen, astute,
       shrewd, perspicacious, sagacious, sage,
       wise, etc.

Exercise 4

*

Exercise 5

(a) An *italicized* word is one printed in "Italian" type, in
    which the letters slope to the right.
(b) A rivulet is a small river or stream.
(c) If the usual freight carried by a ship were slight
    enough to be held in the hand, the steamship line
    would be bankrupt.
(d) Because most people prefer to do what they want

---

* A key to this section defeats it's purpose. If a key becomes
indispensable, use a large dictionary. So with other omitted keys.

rather than to do required work.

(e) Because the habit of not giving up is universally considered a virtue.

(f) Because it is his duty to be actively watchful.

(g) It falls down.

(h) Because *endurance* implies personal strength rather than weakness.

(i) Because they are hateful.

(j) Because strange, mysterious sounds usually frighten us rather than amuse us.

Exercise 6

proboscis—tubular mouth

frothy—foamy

obstinacy—stubbornness

portmanteau—traveling-bag

memorandum—a note or record written down to aid the memory

diligently—industriously

reproof—rebuke, correction

curtsy—a bodily gesture of respectful greeting

survey—examination, inspection

fawn—a young deer

Exercise 7

industrious—hard-working

erroneous—wrong

elevated—high

apprehensive—fearful
cordial—hearty
informal—without ceremony
monotonous—not varying

Exercise 8

(a) splash
(b) rattle
(c) clang; tinkle
(d) babble or ripple

Exercise 9

(c) an entertaining, amusing, dramatic, well-directed, well-acted, intelligently conceived, breathless, exciting, forceful moving- picture; an exciting, well-played, dramatic, stirring baseball game; a tasty, satisfying, well-planned, well-thought-out, skillfully served, pleasant, pleasurable, delicious dinner; a diverting, amusing, funny, gay, delightful, pleasant party.

Exercise 10

(a) Because a culprit is a criminal or wrong doer.
(b) Because a crisis is a turning- point or decisive event.
(c) A tennis racket and a lute are somewhat similar in shape when viewed face on, and both have strings.
(d) Bones.

(e) One, the monarch himself

(f) He reveals it.

(g) The wheels of the train would leave the rails, and as a consequence the train would probably be wrecked.

(h) Because the dog with rabies is a mad dog.

(i) Because the group of persons responsible for making the laws of a state or country must be honest and conscientious if they are to perform effectively the task for which they are appointed.

Exercise 11

(a) A receptacle is a container.
Receptive—ready or able to receive ideas, suggestions, impressions, etc; "He was in a receptive mood."

(b) having to do with the voice
one's calling or occupation
list or stock of words
noisy, shouting, clamorous

(c) having to do with life
strength, power to live, liveliness
a special nourishing substance for the body, necessary to keep it in good health
inner parts of the body necessary to its life

(d) *responsive*—answering, easily responding, easily affected or moved, containing replies or responses ("responsive reading")

(e) *naturalize*—admit to citizenship, bring into common and natural usage in a new place, make at home in another country.

Exercise 12

repentance—regret

implored—begged

remorse—deep regret

depose—forcibly eject (from some position, such as a
    kingship)

affliction—pain, distress

tidings—news, information

amends—compensation, repayment

contrived—managed, planned

diligence—industry

antidote—remedy

Exercise 13

(a) terrified

(b) cautious

(c) heavy; because a ponderous burden is heavier and
    more bulky.

(d) *Strong* means "having strength"; *powerful* means
    "having great strength." *Powerful* is clearly the more
    appropriate adjective for describing an elephant.

(e) A person who strives, tries harder

(f) In this choice between two evils, the curious friend is
    to be preferred. He is interested and would like to
    know; but the inquisitive friend will have no scruples
    about prying and intruding into your affairs.

(g) In such a situation an eager friend would be more of
    a spirited companion than a merely willing one.

Exercise 15

(a) Because the chief purpose in taking food is to nourish the body.

(b) Because a huge rock is too ponderous to be thrown.

(c) Because children are not so likely, even in these days of child movie-stars, to become as famous as adults.

(d) Because an invoice is a bill; most people would rather be in a position of collecting money than paying it.

(e) The jugular vein is in the neck.

(f) A paragon is a model of excellence or perfection. It is a matter of personal taste whether one would or would not care to be such a person.

(g) Because they are too deep to be fathomed, or measured.

(h) He is accused of some crime by a court of law. The word is pronounced as if it were spelled *indite*. (*Indite*, however, is a word of another meaning; one indites a letter when he writes or composes it.)

(i) Because a pentagon is a five-sided, two-dimensional figure.

(j) Because *locomotion* means "travel," "movement," "act of moving."

Exercise 16

abominable—detestable
magistrate—judge
incivility—rudeness
effectual—effective, result-getting

routed—forced, driven
suffice—be enough
noggin—small drink
cove—small bay or inlet
miscellany—collection of miscellaneous articles
repugnance—abhorrence, dislike
>   (It is obviously difficult to improve upon
>   Stevenson's wording.)

Exercise 17

bandit—robber
contentment—happiness
frenzy—excitement
ally—associate
allusion—indirect reference
coronation—crowning
lute—stringed musical instrument
regent—substitute ruler
infidel—unbeliever
immensity—vastness

Exercise 18

*Alarum, scream, shriek, clamorous, appeal, clang,
clash, roar, twanging, clanging, jangling, wrangling*;
other words like *bells, turbulency, startled, tune,* and
so on, add to the general onomatopoetic effect.

Moan, murmuring, pipe, sing, pattering, clashed,

clanged, rang, are the most obvious imitative words; even more effective are *myriads, rivulets, hurrying, doves, immemorial, elms, innumerable, bees, calm, morn, dry, chasms, based, sharp-smitten, dint,* and many others which in their respective passages suggest the sounds of prattling rivulets, moaning doves, and murmuring bees, singing linnets, a calm morning, and the clang and clash of armor upon a rocky cliff.

Exercise 19

(a) unhappy, unsuccessful . . . poor, weak, backward . . . poor, disobedient, unfortunate, discourteous

(b) steep, dangerous . . . sharp, blind, dangerous . . . fatal, unfortunate, serious

(c) poor, unskillful, reckless, clumsy . . . heavy, furious

Exercise 20

(a) Because the government is not appointed by the people who live under it.

(b) He wears a surplice, a broad-sleeved white gown.

(c) If it is not legible, it cannot be read.

(d) Because an attorney is a lawyer, of little help in the curing of illnesses.

(e) The answer to this question depends upon where you live. In New York, snow is exceptional from spring to autumn.

(f) Washington

(g) *Infectious* means "catching," "apt to spread." When someone has a disease, others may catch it if it is infectious; when someone laughs heartily, others are likely to "catch" his merriment and to begin laughing too.

(h) Because the cornea is the outside coating of the eye.

(i) Because a binnacle, being a box designed to hold a ship's compass at about table-height, is lower then a pinnacle.

Exercise 21

(a) *Annual* means yearly.

An annuity is a yearly payment of money.

Annals are historical records, usually kept year to year.

(b) *Erratic* means "queer," "irregular."

Errant means "wandering"; a knight-errant is one who wanders about looking for an adventure.

(c) A quest is a search or hunt.

Questionable means "open to question or debate," doubtful.

A query is a question or inquiry.

A questionnaire is a list of questions.

(d) Shortening is butter, lard, etc. added to dough.

(e) A profiteer is a person who makes an unfair profit by unscrupulously exploiting the public.

Exercise 22

rudiments—fundamentals
infested—disturbed, troubled in large numbers.
melancholy—sad
indistinct—indefinite
accusations—charges
fancy—imagination
malignant—malicious, very evil
reconciled—made satisfied with
abhorrence—detestation, hatred
embarkation—getting on a ship and sailing

Exercise 23

Church—temple, chapel, mosque, synagogue
Witchcraft—sorcery, magic, witchery, enchantment
Ghost—specter, phantom, apparition, spirit
Reward—recompense, remuneration, indemnity,
        compensation
Villain—knave, rogue, rascal, blackguard

Exercise 25

See the Keys to the Vocabulary Tests page 178.

Exercise 26

vermin—injurious, destructive, troublesome
        creatures like fleas, rat, and lice.
vats—tanks, large tubs

corporation—group of persons legally authorized to
        do business as if they were a single
        person.
consternation—fear, dismay
ribald—coarse, irreverent, offensive fellow
vesture—clothing
piebald—with spots of two colors
alien—foreign
ascribe to—explain by, assign to
subterraneous—underground

Exercise 27

fraudulent—dishonest
slothful—lazy
dumfounded—astounded
pliable—flexible
squalid—filthy
pecuniary—financial
avaricious—greedy
maroon—dark red
mongrel—of mixed breed
precipitous—very steep

Exercise 28

(b) Consider *zest, wrath, triumphant, scrutinize,
    meticulous, pompous, horror, terror, quiver,
    shiver, scintillate*, and *pout*.

Exercise 29

(a) slothful, indolent
(b) terrified
(c) indigent, penniless, poverty-stricken
(d) sparkling
(e) ridiculous, hilarious
(f) precipitous
(g) bitter, frigid, freezing
(h) corpulent, obese
(i) sanguine, optimistic
(j) filthy, squalid

Exercise 30

(a) Because a hawser is a thick rope for mooring a ship.
(b) You would feel flattered because *pellucid* means "very clear."
(c) Yes
(d) Because a hogshead is a large cask.
(e) Because the zenith is the highest point in the heavens, directly overhead.
(f) Because *to yaw* means to leave the straight course, thereby causing the boat to travel a longer distance.
(g) By heart, without thinking of the meaning.
(h) Because tariffs are taxes which increase the cost of goods to the purchaser.
(j) Yes

The Growing Vocabulary

Exercise 31

(a) A myth is a legend or an invented story. Mythology is the study of myths, or myths collected and considered together; *mythological* is the adjective corresponding to *mythology*. *Mythical* means "like a myth," "in or of a myth," not real, fictitious.

(b) Merit is worth or value. *Merited* means "deserved." *Meritorious* means "worthy," "deserving."

(c) A prospect is a view, scene, outlook, etc. *Prospective* means "future," "expected," "probable." A *prospector* is a man who searches for gold or other valuable natural resources. A *prospectus* is a printed advertisement describing the "prospects" or outlook for an enterprise or undertaking.

(d) To stupefy is to render dull or unconscious. Stupefaction is stupor, amazement.

(e) A hypocrite is a person who pretends to be what he is not, especially in matters of religion and virtue. Uriah Heep (*David Copperfield*) is a hypocrite. *Hypocrisy* is the name of the quality possessed by hypocrites. *Hypocritical* is the adjective describing such a person or his actions.

(f) *Precipitate* has many meanings; see the dictionary. *Precipitous* means "very steep," "like a precipice." Precipitation is hurry, haste, rainfall, etc. See the dictionary for the many meanings of this word.

A precipitant is a substance that causes another substance dissolved in a liquid to appear in solid form, the adjective *precipitant* means "falling headlong," "rash," "sudden."

Exercise 32

obsequious—servile, overly polite
conciliating—obliging, over-agreeable
shrews—termagants
insuperable—unconquerable
aversion—dislike
fecundity—productiveness, fertility
voluminous—bulky, huge
coquettes—flirts
vigilant—very watchful
censors—supervisors, critics, judges
duenna—chaperone
prudent—discreet
inexorably—unyieldingly
decorous—well-behaved, dignified
superannuated—old, retired because of age

Exercise 33

(a) fat
(b) inestimable
(c) hate
(d) comfort
(e) round
(f) angered
(g) abandonment
(h) rest
(i) inducing
(j) competent

The Growing Vocabulary

Exercise 34

T T F F T F T F T F

Exercise 35

seclude—seclusion
convert—conversion
impeach—impeachment
misconceive—misconception
observe—observation, observance
perplex—perplexity
perturb—perturbation
presume—presumption
pretend—pretension, pretense
recite—recitation, recital
decide—decision
reprehend—reprehension

Exercise 36

pallid—pale, colorless, faded
brawny—muscular
remnants—left-overs, remains
disinherited—dispossessed, deprived of their
                            inheritance
exemplary—model, ideal
ardent—intense, burning
rigidity—stiffness
suspension—temporary stoppage
contingent—indefinite, uncertain, vague, doubtful

vacillation—wavering, unsteadiness of opinion
breach—neglect, breaking
culpable—blamable, blameworthy
behoof—benefit, advantage
implacable—unappeasable, unsootheable
unrelentingly—unyieldingly

Exercise 37

boulder—large rock
legislator — law maker
globule — small sphere
pinafore—apron
savor—flavor
jaunt—short trip
glutton—greedy eater
incumbrance—burden
nucleus—central part
rendezvous—meeting place

Exercise 38

A spectacle is a great public show or display,
    designed primarily to appeal to the eye of the
    beholder. A spectrum is a band of colors, in series,
    made when a beam of light is passed through a
    prism. A specter is a ghost.
A portage is a place in a journey where one *carries* a
    boat or a canoe; a portmanteau is a satchel designed
    to be *carried*.

The Growing Vocabulary

The auditory nerves lead from ear to brain; an
   inaudible sound cannot be heard; a radio audition
   is a trial-hearing given a singer or musician; an
   auditor at a lecture is a listener.
A knight-errant rides about in search of adventure; he
   "wanders" rather than pursues a premeditated course.
   When a person errs, he wanders from the correct path
   and consequently makes a mistake or error.

Exercise 39

(a) speed, hasten, spurt, sprint, fly, post, scuttle, race,
   rush, scurry, whiz, etc.
(b) crawl, lumber, plod, inch, drift, trudge, creep, limp, etc.
(c) sprint, walk, toddle totter, limp, strut, etc.
(d) *Loiter* seems the slowest word. Do you agree?
(e) Speed, sweep, rush, dash, post? Which do *you* think?
(f) *Flow, stream, sweep, rush, glide* apply to the
   motion of water or air.
(g) lag, plod, drag, trudge, stagger, struggle along, etc.
(h) float, cruise, voyage, and possibly others.

Exercise 40

(a) No. Rest and good food strengthen rather weaken.
(b) A dull-bluish bruise.
(c) Because spurious money is false or counterfeit.
(d) Docility means "teachableness," "obedience."
   Most people desire their dogs to be docile.
(e) No. A languorous athlete is too lacking in energy,

too listless, to distinguish himself in a contest.
(f) Because a rebus is a sort of puzzle in which
pictures suggest syllables or words.
(g) Because obsequies are funeral ceremonies.
(h) Concavity
(i) No. Furtive means "sneaky," "evasive," "sly,"
"stealthy."
(j) No, because a mausoleum is a tomb.

Exercise 41

(a) Oratory is the art of speaking in public.
An oracle is a wise person who can give answers
to difficult questions. See the dictionary.
An oratorio is a kind of religious opera which
lacks, however, the elements of action, scenery,
and costume.
(b) *Remit* means "to send money to someone," to
pardon, to decrease. See the dictionary for the
various meanings of this useful word.
A remittance is the sending of money to
someone, or the money so sent.
Remission is pardon, forgiveness, or reduction.
Remiss means careless, forgetful, negligent.
Remissness is carelessness, negligence.
(d) See the Key to Section 38.

Exercise 42

conjecture—guess
privy to—secretly aware of
harassed—worried, bothered
distracted—confused, disturbed
machinations—schemings, evil plottings
usurper—person who seizes power or position by force
acclamations—shouts of praise and applause
impregnable—not to be taken by force
scrupulous—regardful of what is right in every detail
inordinate—excessive
usurer—extortionate moneylender
amassed—piled up, gathered
pretensions—claims
prevail upon—persuade
revoke—recall, remit

Exercise 43

(a) happiness
(b) empty
(c) skillful
(d) half circle
(e) incredible
(f) living place
(g) abandoned
(h) prison cell
(i) lively
(j) pirates

Exercise 44

F F F F T F T T T T
(1) Superlative beauty is beauty of the highest kind,
certainly not possessed by apes.

(2) Optimistic persons are usually sanguine and hopeful.

(3) *Convalescent* means "recovering from illness."

(4) A coot is a species of bird that can swim and dive in the water.

(6) *Garrulous* means talkative.

(7) *Voracious* means greedy.

Exercise 45

deception—deceptive
scandal—scandalous
book—bookish
improbability—improbable
moment—momentary, momentous
enigma — enigmatic
nucleus — nuclear
period — periodic, periodical
municipality—municipal
profit—profitable
profundity—profound
reception—receptive
revolution—revolutionary
simplicity—simple

Exercise 46

emulating—imitating, copying
razed—torn down
avidity—eagerness

abstinence—refraining
environs—neighborhood, surroundings
scathed—harmed, injured, hurt
allegory—story told to teach or explain something
implacable—unappeasable, unyielding
palsied—paralyzed
artifice—clever trick
imprecations—curses
inexplicable—unexplainable
akimbo—with her hands on her hips
termagant—shrew, scolding woman
precursor—forerunner, preliminary

Exercise 47

to foreknow—to know ahead of time
to incite—to stir up
to maraud—to plunder
to particularize—to mention individually
to reminisce—to recall past happenings
to segregate—to set apart from the others
to snivel—to whine; to whimper
to vilify—to speak evil of
to desecrate—to profane
to flinch—to shrink from
to perforate—to make holes in

Exercise 48

(a) A tangent to a circle is a line that touches the circle at one point.

(b) Canada and Mexico are both contiguous to the United States; both touch it.

(c) An orange is tangible or "touchable"; honor is intangible.

(d) A house is a habitation.

(e) Animals or plants.

(f) Applause which comes again and again is recurrent.

(g) A courier "runs" in the sense that he hurries in the carrying of a message.

(h) Dormant abilities are abilities still asleep in a person and as yet unrevealed or undeveloped.

(i) A vocation is one's calling ; an avocation is one's hobby.

(j) A vocation is the task to which one is "called"; an avocation is an activity that calls one away from his vocation.

Exercise 49

(a) The funny part of the situation . . . about how much he does . . . really does nothing.

(b) It is interesting to compare . . . and their doings.

(c) The fact . . . ship.

(d) hook . . . your chief interests.

(e) When he plays basketball, a player should try to put . . . back boards.

(f) The characteristic . . .

Exercise 50

See the Keys to the Vocabulary Tests page 178.

Exercise 51

(a) to happen before (something else)
   happening before; something happening before
   before noon
   a room which one enters before entering another,
   like the waiting room of a doctor's office
   occurring before the Flood, ancient
(b) to sail around (the earth)
   distance around (a circle)
   a roundabout, indirect way of speaking
   to draw a line around
(c) a passage under the ground
   a boat designed to sail under the sea
   under the level of consciousness, unconscious
   to lease property to someone which the lessor has
   already leased from another person. The idea is
   that if A rents property to B, who then in turn
   rents it to C, A is "above" B, and C is "under" B.
   to put under water
   underground
(d) opposition against slavery
   a substance useful against infection
   opposed to ("against") society and its laws

a substance useful against disease
(e) an airplane with one plane; i.e.; with one pair of wings
a ruler who rules singly or alone
part spoken by single actor
a single eyeglass
initials combined into a single design
a single stone or rock
insanity on one subject only
a single syllable

Exercise 52

(a) change
(b) mournful
(c) deceased, dead
(d) praises
(e) liveliness
(f) *conjugal bereavement*—loss of his wife by death
(g) staleness, commonplaceness
(h) a strange fancy
tear bottle
burial
(i) searching
(j) of the ruler of a family or tribe
(k) prejudiced
archbishop or highest ranking bishop

Exercise 53

happy—unhappy, miserable, sad, depressed, gloomy,
  etc.
stupid—smart, astute, shrewd, intelligent, clever, etc.
new—old, ancient, aged, antediluvian, decrepit, etc.
easy—hard, difficult, arduous, etc.
sensible—foolish, unwise, silly, foolhardy, etc.
wrong—correct, right, accurate, proper, etc.
slow—fast, speedy, rapid, hurried, etc.
big—little, small, minute, tiny, microscopic, etc.

Exercise 54

F T F T F T F T F T

Exercise 55

(a) Because to *felicitate* means to congratulate.
(b) No; malnutrition is poor or insufficient
  nourishment.
(c) So small as to be almost non-existent.
(d) Yes; *obviate* means remove.
(e) A morion is a helmet, a moron is an adult of
  feeble intellect.
(f) No, *sardonic* means bitterly sarcastic, scornful.
(g) Yes; a sedative quiets the nerves.
(h) Yes; an encumbrance is a hindrance.
(i) He tries hard. *Herculean* accented on the second
  syllable.
(j) Because *predilection* means preference.

Exercise 56

1. lost his head—became confused
2. made after—pursued
3. gave himself away—betrayed himself
4. hung upon—paid close attention to
5. put down—suppressed
6. takes after—resembles
7. put by—saved
8. to take in
9. He is very much like one of his parents.
10. to come to

Exercise 57

clarity—clearness
curvet—lcap of a horse
fallow—land left unseeded
marchioness—wife of a marquis
curvature—curving
mandate—command
obduracy—stubbornness; hardness of heart
pigment—coloring matter
queue—pigtail
curriculum—course of study
ingot—bar of metal
schism—division into hostile groups

The Growing Vocabulary

Etymological means dealing with the origin and history of words.

(a) *dicere* means to say, or to speak.

(b) *ject-* is connected with the idea of throwing, hurling.

(c) *ponere* means to put, to place

(d) *valere* means to be in good health, to be valuable, to be strong.

Exercise 60

(a) The diphthong is *oi*; a diphthong is two vowels pronounced together.

(b) Yes. *Incongruous* means inconsistent, out of place. A high silk hat worn by a laboring man while at work is incongruous.

(c) Because plagiarism is the theft of another's ideas, words, etc.

(d) Because to obtain money by threatening people is to deserve punishment.

(e) A surgeon uses forceps, which are small tongs or pincers.

(f) Because an axiom is a statement so obviously true that no proof seems necessary. "A straight line is the shortest distance between two points" is an axiom.

(g) Monotheistic; *polytheistic* means "having many gods," whereas *monotheistic* means "having one god."

(h) Clement (mild, gentle, pleasant) weather is preferable.

(i) Because *flaccid* means limp, drooping. Such a balloon
doubtless contains insufficient gas to keep it afloat.
(j) Yes; *efficacious* means effective.

Exercise 61

(a) equally distant (from some point) with equal sides.
balance (implying equal weight on both or all sides)
even, equal balance
an imaginary line about the earth, equidistant
from the poles
equal in value
(b) a two-wheeled vehicle
two times a year
speaking two languages
marriage to two wives or husbands
twice a month, or once every two months
(c) after the war
people who live after us; descendants
a back door or gate
happening after death, born after death (of its father)
an examination after death
an addition to a letter after the signature
(d) across the Atlantic
across the continent
part of a cruciform church that crosses the main part
to pierce through
journey across (consult the dictionary)
letting light come through

(e) a word consisting of many syllables
a school where many arts and sciences are taught
marriage with many wives or husbands
a geometric figure with many sides

Exercise 62

urging—instigation
agreement—concurrence
opposing groups of persons—factions
student of chemical magic—alchemist
made known—intimated
almost too much kindness—indulgence
unlimited—unbounded
unwise—injudicious
boldly rude—insolent
behavior—demeanor
devotee—votary
sarcastic—caustic
accustomed—habituated
diligent—assiduous
increasing—enhancing

Exercise 63

destroy—create
contract—expand
attract—repel
follow—precede
hasten—loiter

praise—censure
exult—grieve deeply
concentrate—diffuse
anathematize—bless
cleave—join together

Exercise 64

F T T F T T T F T F

Exercise 65

(a) Because bacteriology is the study of the germs
which cause disease.

(b) Because genealogical trees are charts showing
family relationships.

(c) No; to be henpecked is merely to be ruled by one's wife.

(d) An impassive person is too listless and lacking
energy to be restless or impatient.

(e) A politician, who must scheme and must
counteract the schemes of others, cannot afford to
be artless, childlike, or naive

(f) It was stolen.

(g) It is babyish to whimper when slightly injured.

(h) Sheep; *gregarious* means "living in flocks."

(i) No; the purlieus of New York City lie in its
immediate neighborhood.

(j) A *prefix* is a syllable attached to the beginning of a word;
a suffix is a syllable attached to the end of a word.

Exercise 66

1. steer clear of—avoid
2. keeps abreast of—keeps informed of
3. knows the ropes—has a knowledge of how to get along
4. to ferret out—discover
5. beats about the bush—avoids coming to the point

6. a bolt from the blue—a complete surprise
7. laid his cards on the table—was open in his dealings
8. set her face against—opposed
9. pull through—recover
10. gets on well with—is congenial and friendly with
11. getting on in years—growing old
12. made bold—had the courage to do it
13. keep him under your eye—watch him
14. straight from the shoulder—frankly
15. held forth at great length—talked lengthily

Exercise 67

corpulence—fatness
comfit—piece of candy
modicum—small quantity
scarab—beetle
colloquy—conversation
shibboleth—watchword
elucidation—explanation
emir—Arab chieftain
imposture—deception, fraud
inadequacy—insufficiency
jaunt—short trip
nonchalance—unconcerned

Exercise 68

(a) To proceed is to go ahead; to recede is to go back
(b) The king goes first. Notice that *precedence* is

accented on the second syllable.

(c) A tractable horse is easily managed, an intractable horse is not.

(d) He withdraws it, or takes it back.

(e) A potent criminal is worse because he is already powerful; a potential criminal is capable of developing into a criminal.

(f) A potentate is a powerful ruler.

Exercise 70

(a) No, because *nebulous* means hazy, vague indefinite.

(b) A rectangle is a parallelogram; that is, its opposite sides are parallel; a triangle is not a parallelogram.

(c) A shellfish (like and oyster) needs a strong muscle to close its shell against an enemy.

(d) Any animal that preys upon other animals is called predatory. Tigers, pumas, lions, hawks, eagles, and owls are predatory.

(e) Because a puma is a large wildcat, whereas a pundit is a learned scholar.

(f) A climate that enfeebles naturally causes the people living in it to decline in vigor.

(g) This statement is scarcely debatable because there are no arguments to prove that worms have feathers. A debatable subject must have two sides to it.

(h) Because a panacea is a remedy for all diseases; the finding of a genuine panacea would render valueless most of a druggist's stock.

The Growing Vocabulary

(a) self-written biography
   a ruler who has entire authority himself
   the name of a person written by himself
   a machine that moves itself
   self governing

(b) blessing ("well-saying")
   kindly ("well-wishing")
   one who receives anything designed for his
   benefit or well-being

(c) the distance around the boundary of any surface,
   like a square or circle
   an instrument which enables a man in a
   submarine or a trench to look around while hidden
   outside boundary; synonymous with *circumference*
   and *perimeter*

(d) to move backward
   a view backward, a survey of the past

(e) an instrument for seeing objects far off
   an electrical device for seeing objects far off
   to send a written message afar by electrical
   means
   to send a spoken message afar by electrical
   means
   communication by separate minds ("from afar")
   by means not clearly understood by scientific
   investigators

Exercise 72

(a) aimless wandering
(b) a child born after the death of my father
(c) exclaiming
(d) overcoat
(e) a yellowish-buff cotton cloth
(f) curses
(g) wrongdoings . . . silently
(h) secret
(i) financial . . . greedy
(j) made permanent . . . trickeries
(k) concluding summary, conclusion
(l) prove these accusations by definite evidence

Exercise 73

(a) generous
(b) antagonism
(c) traitorous, treasonable, false
(d) the affirmative
(e) valorous, intrepid, audacious

Exercise 74

F T T T F T F T T F F F T F F

Exercise 75

See the Keys to the Vocabulary Tests, page 179.

Exercise 76

1. warn the cook that she is to be discharged
2. made many a man conceited
3. people cry "fire!" . . . join in
4. deceived
5. rejoices at, laughs at
6. getting oneself into a fight with
7. impressed him........frightened him
8. attacked
9. drunk . . . out of his senses
10. catch him

Exercise 78

(a) It is the blessing ("well-saying")
(b) Benefactors, because most people would prefer doing well to doing ill.
(c) You would doubtless rather have a benevolent ("well-wishing") father than a malevolent ("ill-wishing") one.
(d) One whose sides are of equal length
(e) Yes, because equanimity is calmness of mind, poise.
(f) *Biannual* means "twice a year"; *biennial* means "every two years."

Exercise 79

(a) He makes up words to please himself rather than following the words of the play.
(b) In 1939, England and France; in 1940 Germany

and Italy in 1941, . . . ?

(c) Mark Twain

(d) They wish to keep conditions the same, without changes or the introduction of new ideas.

(e) None at all.

(f) *Blitzkrieg, straf, lbensraum, ersatz, heil, fürher, verboten, c'est la guerre, après la guerre, camion.*

Exercise 80

(a) An azalea, because such a flower-bearing bush is preferable in a garden to a large and dangerous snake like the anaconda.

(b) A snarled fish-line is tangled.

(c) To hector is to bully; small boys seldom bully football captains.

(d) Conceited people who look down upon those in lower social positions.

(e) Blarney is flattering, persuasive talk; politicians find it useful in winning votes.

(f) Succotash is a mixture of corn and beans, balderdash is nonsensical talk.

(g) a policeman

(h) Because they are figures carved from stone and are consequently unable to communicate by talking or other means.

(i) Chesterton was a writer skilled in making statements apparently false but actually true, or partly true. "The child is father to the man" is a paradox.

(j) an epigram

Exercise 81

Use your dictionary!

Exercise 82

(a) Yes. Amphibious means "living both on land and in the water."

(b) Monogamy.

(c) An instrument for looking at and examining the sun.

(d) An instrument for measuring small distances or dimensions.

Exercise 83

(a) He refuses to endorse it.

(b) collaborator

(c) genuine

(d) *Infamous* means disgraceful, shamefully bad, well known for wickedness. An accurate antonym of *famous* is *obscure* or *little-known*.

(e) The following words form antonyms by dropping the prefix in-; *inaccessible, inarticulate, incompatible* and *incredulous*.

inaccessible—very hard to get at

inadvertent—negligent, accidental, not done on purpose

inarticulate—unable to speak; not jointed; not distinct

incapacitate—to make incapable

incense—to anger; sweet smelling smoke

incompatible—not agreeable

incredulous—unable to believe, doubting

indigent—poor, penniless

(g) *Habitable* and *inhabitable* are synonyms; so are the other pair of words listed here. *Invaluable* means priceless, too valuable to be estimated.

Exercise 84

T T F T T T T T F T T F F F T F T F T T

3. A flamingo is a large, pinkish water-bird with long legs and neck.

9. Dyspepsia is poor digestion.

12. *Abscond* means "go away secretly and hide."

13. Destitution is great poverty.

14. Gentians are blue flowers growing usually in hilly country.

16. Glass is transparent because one can see through it; paper is translucent because one can see light through it, a brick is opaque because one can see nothing through it, not even light.

18. The solar plexus is a concentration of nerves near the stomach.

Exercise 85

episode
sacrilege
irresolution, irresoluteness
treason
monosyllable
intuition
gymnastics, gymnasium

irascibility
morbidity, morbidness
prescience
rusticity
literacy, literateness
ebullience, ebulliency
stealth, stealthiness

The Growing Vocabulary

Exercise 86

1. f	2. j	3. l	4. q
5. h	6. u	7. b	8. p
9. s	10.a	11.c	12.v
13.i	14.m	15.w	

Exercise 87

sweets—candy

wash-rags—face-clothes

mackintoshes—raincoats

boots—high shoes

shoes—low shoes

galoshes—rubbers

counterpanes—bedspreads

porridge—cereal

biscuits—crackers

pudding—dessert

tinned—canned

tap—faucet

tram—streetcar

motor-car—automobile

Underground—the subway

railway-lines—tracks

sleepers—ties

playtime—recess

knuckle-bones—jacks

skipping rope—jumping rope

cinema—movies

Exercise 89

(a) They urged people to enjoy life day by day as they lived it, not to look for happiness in the future.

(b) *Gauche* comes to mean "clumsy" or "tactless" because left-handed people are supposed to be less skillful then right-handed people.

(c) It opens in the middle of the story, returning later to narrate the beginning.

(d) *Prima facie* evidence is such evidence as at first

glance reveals that a murder has been committed: a dead body, a pistol containing one or more discharged cartridges lying on the floor nearby, footprints on the rug, etc.

(e) Any rare or nonexistent creature can be called a *rara avis*.

(f) Because *sang froid* is coolness, presence of mind.

(g) At an indefinite time in the future, as yet undetermined.

Exercise 90

(a) People raise an outcry, such as "Stop thief!"

(b) To cogitate is to think.

(c) *Literate* means able to read.

(d) Because procrastination is the habit of delaying, of putting off till tomorrow what can be done today; it is a habit which frequently leads to waste of time.

(e) Because a longshoreman is a man employed on wharves to load ships; he does not sail with the ships.

(f) Because a layman, being a person who belongs to no profession, is not a surgeon or physician.

(g) Because a pandemonium is a place of wild noise and confusion.

(h) Because *posterity* is a word used of people who will live in the future, our descendants; we can inherit only from those who have lived before us, our progenitors, ancestors, forefathers.

(i) Because *simous* means twisting, turning, winding.

(j) Because to synchronize two watches is merely to

set them to agree in time.

(k) Because *magna cum laude* means "with great praise." whereas *cum laude* means merely "with praise."

(l) *Armor-propre* is self respect; it is considered a highly desirable quality.

(m) Because a rhombus is by definition a parallelogram with equal sides that is not a square. A diamond shape is a *rhombus*.

(n) *Spouse*.

(o) Because a decapitation is the cutting off of a person's head.

Exercise 91

Use your dictionary.

Exercise 92

Optometry is the science of measuring human eyesight for the determination of proper glasses. *Pathology* is the science of disease from which people suffer; *antipathy* is dislike, a feeling against someone or something which causes one to suffer; *pathos* is that quality in a situation, etc. which arouses the pity of the observer. *Petrography* is the study and recording of facts about rocks; *to petrify* is to turn into rock; *petroleum* is oil found in the earth, among rocks; *petrology* is the study of rocks. *Hydrodynamics* concern water-power; a *hydrometer* is a device for measuring the densities of liquids, like water; *hydroelectric* concerns the generation of electricity from water-power; *hydraulic* means "having to do with water in motion." An *anachronism* is an event, person, etc. ascribed to a time to which it does not belong; *isochronous* means "having the same time." A *demagogue* makes a special appeal to the common people.

The meanings of the other words are probably familiar. If not, use a dictionary.

Exercise 93

(a) to become excited and confused
   to reach a crisis
   to talk a great deal
   to suggest an idea to someone
   to be delirious
   to become conceited

(b) to head off; over one's head; to give someone his head; to keep one's head, etc.

(c) to have the boldness to
   to oppose
   to overcome someone by one's mere presence
   to see something through to the end
   to interpret favorably

(d) to concentrate on looking
   to watch, to look out for
   to be able to distinguish
   to ignore deliberately
   tit for tat, punishment exactly equal to the offense
   hidden or obscure meanings

The Growing Vocabulary

Exercise 94

T F T F F F T T F F T F F T F F T T F T

2) *Verdant* means green.
4) Tantrums are fits of ill humor.
5) Decorum is dignified, proper behavior
6) A benefactor is a person who helps others,
9) *Flamboyant* means "gorgeous in color."
10) A copeck is a Russian coin.
12) A parasite is a person, animal, or plant that lives on the strength of another; a hypocrite is a pretender.
13) *Comely* means "lovely"; *uncouth* means "crude, unpleasant."
15) To precipitate a war is to bring it about.
16) A vanguard is the front part of an army.
19) A stalactite hangs like an icicle; a stalagmite projects upward; both are formations of lime caused by dripping water in caves.

Exercise 95

jeopardy
ostracism
preponderance, preponderation
eulogy
disparagement
laceration

rhapsody
gibberish, gibbering
liquefaction
protrusion
purveyance
reciprocation, reciprocity

Exercise 97

grown ups—adults
sea—ocean
ill—sick
chemist shop—drugstore
tea cloths—dish-towels
draper's—fabric store
shop assistants—clerks
flannelette—soft cotton cloth
calico—printed cloth
cotton wool—raw cotton
tacking—basting
reel of cotton—spool of thread
smallwear—notions
bottom-drawer—hope chest
greengrocer—vegetable man
corn—grain
maize—corn
waistcoats—vests
public house—tavern

Exercise 98

I

insane—demented
predictions—prognostication
educated—erudite
untrue—fallacious
black—sable
salacious—obscene

II

chic—stylish
ennui—weariness
legerdemain—prestidigitation
sub rosa—confidentially
vis-a`-vis—face to face
scullion—kitchen servant

III

wraith—specter
wheedle—coax
evaporating rapidly—volatile
revile—vituperate
of great size—voluminous
glassy—vitreous

IV

ulster—overcoat
trice—very short time
throe—agony
purveyance—provisions

major-domo—steward
germinate—sprout

V

viscous—sticky
trepidation—fear
ewer—water pitcher
gratuitous—free
violent storm—typhoon
irksome—tedious

VI

swollen—turgid
ghoul—grave-robber
unwise—injudicious
matriculate—enroll as a student
speak evil of—vilify
moiety—part

VII

vertex—highest point
petulant—peevish
refulgent—splendid
inequitable—unfair
scurrilous—abusive
sear—withered

VIII

reduplicate—repeat
secrete—hide

verbosity—wordiness
sirocco—hot, dry wind
sterility—barrenness
feeler—tentacle

IX

mediocre—of ordinary quality
vassalage—servitude
prowess—bravery
pusillanimous—cowardly
profligate—very wicked
risible—laughable

Exercise 100

See the keys to the Vocabulary Tests, page 179.

The End